"A really excellent, thorough, practical, entertaining and inspiring guide to generating great conversations with strangers, co-workers, friends, family, neighbours – anyone and everyone! It's wonderfully helpful on the mysteries of everyday, easy small talk, as well as of the deeper, more personal, heartfelt human connections we want to create in our lives. There are lots of useful example scripts and opening lines, activities and experiments for all occasions – and there's lots of encouragement along the way to take your conversational repertoire, your self-awareness, self-confidence and enjoyment in life to whole new levels."
Judith Lowe, PPD Learning Ltd, NLP Training Institute, London

"Whether you need step-by-step instructions for conversation, or more advanced tips, there's a part of this book that will suit you. Warm, intelligent and practical, at times Judy draws in seemingly unconnected skills and ideas, and then shows how much good conversation depends on unexpectedly varied things."
Christopher Miller, Founder, Investment Quotient

"In *The Art of Conversation*, Judy invites us into the inner workings of conversation. Melting the blocks that can prevent real connection, she shows how we can tune into the subtle nuances of the most simple to the more challenging conversations in a way that enriches our relationships and lives. A profound and delightful book that allows you to find and refine your conversational flow."
Clare Russell, your guide to living intuitively and Owner of Metalife Ltd

"Over the last 15 years I have watched hundreds of people learn to speak in public through the Toastmasters organization. Many become good enough to be professional speakers, most at least master the art – once they realize it's a conversation with the audience. But not everyone can master the unprepared conversation with strangers or friends. Learn to get it right with Judy's help."
Jenny Cutler, Founder of Image Counts, Author and Toastmaster

"*The Art of Conversation* does what it says on the cover. It provides the tips and content that makes for great conversations in a world where conversations are worryingly on the decline. The level of detail and understanding of how a conversation works is refreshing! This is definitely one for the recommendations list."
Jackee Holder, Coach, Author and Speaker

"There's much more to simple conversation than we might imagine, and Judy's humor and relaxed style are reflected throughout, making this an engaging and entertaining read. I particularly love the pauses for reflection and Judy's exquisite observations. I would recommend getting a copy of *The Art of Conversation* to discover its secrets for yourself!"
Karen Moxom, Managing Director of The Association for NLP, Author of *The NLP Professional* and publisher of *Rapport*

"Contains lots of great little stories which make the book a very easy read and, more than the stories, there is a lot of really practical advice on how to help your own communication stories so they become chronicles of success. There is

definitely something here for anyone wanting to lift their conversation skills to another level."
Paul Matthews, MD and Founder of People Alchemy Ltd and Author of
Informal Learning at Work: How to Boost Performance in Tough Times

"The skill to converse doesn't come quite as naturally to people (anymore) as they might wish. In the digital world our conversations are often disjointed, and we spend more time alone in merely virtual relationships. Yet creating true connections, one-to-one, is still a great source of happiness. Successful conversations make satisfying relationships and give us hope for human society. Judy Apps' *The Art of Conversation* provides enjoyable help for skilling up – or for checking on the skills we think we have."
Sabine Frank, Director, Platform for Intercultural Europe

"This insightful book reveals the essential elements of powerful fluid conversations. It is for you if you are in any way interested in improving your relationships and in making conversation an enjoyable art and intimate dance."
Steve Nobel, Author, Coach, Writer, ex-director Alternatives, London (2000–2012)

"This insightful and beautifully-written book is quite simply a treasure trove. This book is practical but never boring. It shows how good conversation can be an enjoyable and life-enhancing skill. It helped me to understand how conversation works, how to deal with difficult situations, and what to do to make it even better. Most importantly, it also gave me the motivation, enthusiasm and self-confidence to go out and practice."
Celia Morris MBA Chartered FCIPD, Training and Development Manager at Mott MacDonald

"In *The Art of Conversation* Judy Apps delightfully engages us in a conversation about this most pervasive element of the human experience. Her book masterfully integrates principles of conscious communication into the dance of conversation. In the process we get an abundance of practical insights and methods for becoming an excellent conversationalist across all spheres of life. The writing is engaging, captivating, addressing nuance and subtlety with simultaneous sophistication and simplicity. I enthusiastically recommend this book to anyone dedicated to distinction as a communicator, and to coach and mentor others in that direction."
David Wolf, Ph.D., MCC., Founder and Director of Satvatove Institute School of Transformative Coaching and Author of *Relationships That Work, The Power of Conscious Living*

THE ART OF CONVERSATION

CHANGE YOUR LIFE WITH CONFIDENT COMMUNICATION

Judy Apps

CAPSTONE
A Wiley Brand

© 2014 Judy Apps

Registered office
John Wiley and Sons Ltd, The Atrium, Southern Gate, Chichester, West Sussex, PO19 8SQ, United Kingdom

For details of our global editorial offices, for customer services and for information about how to apply for permission to reuse the copyright material in this book please see our website at www.wiley.com.

Library of Congress Cataloging-in-Publication Data is available

A catalogue record for this book is available from the British Library.

ISBN 978-0-857-08538-2 (hbk)
ISBN 978-0-857-08539-9 (ebk)   ISBN 978-0-857-08540-5 (ebk)

Cover designed by Parent Design

Set in 10/12.5 Rotis Sans Serif Std by Toppan Best-Set Premedia Limited
Printed in Great Britain by TJ International Ltd, Padstow, Cornwall, UK

Angela Champ

CONTENTS

Preface	vii
Acknowledgements	ix
Introduction	1

Part 1: Introducing Conversation — 9
1. The Dance of Conversation — 11
2. Connecting is What Matters Most — 21
3. Getting in the Right State — 49
4. Getting a Conversation Going – The Basics — 65
5. Listening — 79

Part 2: The Power of Conversation — 99
6. Influencing a Conversation — 101
7. Different Kinds of Conversation — 117
8. Expressing Yourself — 155

Part 3: Sailing Through Tricky Waters — 171
9. What to Do If You're Stuck — 173
10. Oiling the Wheels — 179
11. Role Playing — 183
12. Spotting the Games People Play — 187
13. Enjoying Disagreement — 197
14. Confrontation — 201

Part 4: Creative Conversations — 213
15. Changing the World One Conversation at a Time — 215

About the Author	225
Image Credits	227
Index	229

PREFACE

There's nothing more enjoyable than an afternoon with friends, just eating, drinking, chatting and having a good time. We were sitting there, reflecting on just how pleasant it was to talk with close friends and feel heard and understood, when someone remarked:

"Some people just don't *get* conversation, do they? I met an old friend the other day, and she talked to me for almost an hour while I just nodded and made encouraging noises. As she left, my friend said how lovely it was to chat to each other and how interesting the conversation had been. I'd told her nothing at all!"

We all recognized the scenario, and laughed. Our conversation turned to various conversational experiences; good, bad and often hilarious.

Frank turned to me. "Someone should write a book about the art of conversation," he said.

Thanks Frank. Here it is.

ACKNOWLEDGEMENTS

I'd like to thank everyone at Capstone, my commissioning editor Holly Bennion and Vicky Kinsman who believed in the project and guided it on its way, Jenny Ng, my wise and patient Development Editor, Production Editor Tessa Allen and all the marketing and sales teams.

I'd also like to thank my supportive family and the good friends with whom I've discussed this huge topic over the years. I'm lucky to have you all in my life.

INTRODUCTION

NORMAL AND EVERYDAY

Conversation! It's the most common thing in the world – so normal, so natural, so everywhere, so everyday. All over the globe, people are talking to each other. "It's good to talk," as the advert says. "Talking, talking happy talk," to quote the song.

Seeing that we all do so much of it, surely we can all *do* conversation? Humans talk to each other – we are essentially social beings; that's what we *do*. I'm pretty sure the caveman had some way of communicating to his mate, "How does that fire-making thing work?" Many of us don't think twice before we open our mouth to communicate – it's the most spontaneous thing in the world.

But *how* we talk, ah, that is the question. Most of us learned how to converse with other people haphazardly through copying the habits of our parents and carers. Most of us didn't learn the subtleties of conversation at school – at least, not formally! We never learned to appreciate the extraordinary potential of conversation, nor how to do it well. The art of conversation is perhaps the most commonly neglected skill on the globe. If you do command the art of conversation when you are young, you have a tremendous advantage in life in all sorts of ways.

The word "conversation" is a humble one. A thesaurus offers a long list of more weighty and impressive words to express the idea of talking to each other. There's discussion, exchange, dialogue, discourse, parley, colloquy . . . You've probably seen books on persuasion, debate, tendering or selling. Governments engage in talks; national envoys handle negotiations; the media cover international summit conferences. But the common ingredient of all these grander concepts is conversation – it's the basic building block of our connection with each other. There aren't many days – depending on your circumstances – that you don't have several conversations! In fact, a day without any conversation probably stands out as an unusual day – a lonely day even.

THE KEY TO MANY DOORS

So if conversation is the basis of human contact, the ability to converse well with people has a lot going for it. Learn to hold a conversation skilfully and you have a magic ingredient for well-being, success and happiness in many areas of your life.

Take relationships: *how* you engage in conversation makes a profound difference to the quality of your connection with other human beings. It's the basis of building new relationships and making new friends. It's how you become intimate with someone. "How did Mary agree to marry you?" I asked a friend. "I engaged her in conversation – I mean, I chatted her up!" came the reply. It's the way you improve your current relationships and understand other people better. It's the way you heal relationships that are not working, whether on a personal or a professional level.

Conversation creates good times too. An entertaining conversation is a source of fun and laughter. Did you ever joke in the playground with school friends or whisper conspiratorially in class? Do you enjoy those special moments of snatched personal conversation by the water cooler at work, or chatting with a stranger in a pub – a place especially conducive to entertaining conversations? You may find out something interesting you didn't know before. You may walk away from a conversation fascinated or amused, moved, enlightened or inspired.

In the workplace, the ability to engage confidently in conversation is a vital, though surprisingly untapped, skill that has the potential to take you far. It eases your relationships with colleagues and bosses. It serves you well in interviews, meetings and reviews. The ability to talk easily with anyone enables you to enjoy networking and make the most of opportunities that come your way. It makes you sound articulate and confident, able to hold your own in debate; it gets you noticed, furthers your career and smoothes your path to promotion.

Skilful conversation helps you to uncover the truth and make wise decisions about people. Then you recruit with discernment and give responsibility to the right people. The best negotiators have highly developed conversational skills. How do you influence and persuade other people of your point of view, or indeed sell them an idea or a product? You'll probably be most successful through engaging them in conversation.

In today's world there are many ways to learn, but it is often said that the best teaching is a conversation with an open channel between teacher and pupil. Lucky is the child who learned good conversation early. "The most influential of all educational factors is the conversation in a child's home," asserted William Temple, inspirational Archbishop of Canterbury during World War II. Excitement and motivation in learning are aroused by live conversation. You may remember a particular schoolteacher who had a major influence on you through inspirational conversation.

Educational discourse goes right back to the Greeks and earlier. Socrates was renowned for his much imitated method of philosophical enquiry. In our own times, some of the most exciting scientific discoveries have been the outcome of conversations between experts of different disciplines. The discovery of DNA, successes in magnetic resonance imaging, chaos theory, radar, human genome sequencing and manned space flight have all been the result of scientists from different disciplines talking to each other, sharing information and sparking ideas off each other. Multidisciplinary conversations have become a major pursuit in universities around the world.

When we look at leaders and politicians, the ability not only to speak articulately but also to engage in robust dialogue is a vital skill, yet given strangely low priority in the state educational system. In policing and the law, fact-finding and interrogating demand a highly skilled command of conversation. On a world scale, conversation between civilizations builds bridges and promotes peace. As the television producer Mark Burnett once said, "I learned first hand that there would simply be no wars if people engaged in real conversation."

Conversation is the basis of the helping and healing professions, counselling, therapy, mentoring and coaching – highly skilled vocations where a good part of the skill lies in the ability to hold a simple conversation with subtlety and intuition.

Good conversational skills can transform every aspect of your world. At its best, it can lead you to experience some of the most rewarding and profound moments of your life. The simplest conversation can hold a hidden thread of the most intimate and beautiful connection . . . if you know the secret.

WHAT THIS BOOK IS AND ISN'T

In this book you'll discover how conversation functions and how to make it work for you. Books already exist on making friends and influencing people, networking for success, holding assertive conversations, difficult conversations, persuasion and much more. We will explore some of these areas too, but if you understand how conversation itself works, and can *do* conversation at it's simplest, you have an invaluable tool to use in every part of your life for pleasure, profit and love. You could choose to read 25 books on 25 different *kinds* of conversations, but the key *is* conversation itself. With this practical knowledge you can do it all!

So explore its hidden parameters and build your self-confidence, starting from here and now.

The first part of the book shows you how conversation works like a dance, with both parties equally engaged. The connection they build between them is key, and I give you lots of hints and tips to help you connect well with people. I offer practical help if you're daunted, nervous, don't know what to say, or ramble and rattle on. I show you how to manage your state, trust yourself and feel more comfortable talking with people. Finally, I introduce you to the practical basics of getting a satisfying conversation going and how to keep the other person interested. Learning how to listen dynamically is an important element, with more to it than meets the eye – or ear!

In the second part of the book you build the skills to be a powerful communicator. You find out how to influence the other person and to direct the talk towards particular outcomes. I introduce you to a powerful method for taking conversation to different levels, so that you are able to move a conversation from everyday comments towards greater understanding and intimacy. You discover how to express yourself more powerfully and authentically with voice and body language, and how to use intellect, feeling and intuition as you speak.

In the third part of the book you take conversation out into your daily life to deal with common difficulties you might encounter, such as getting stuck or dealing with people who play mind games. You discover valuable skills for disagreeing with people without losing connection, and for confronting others when necessary.

This leads us in the final part to explore the beautiful depths and possibilities of communication with each other. There are conversations that changed history and changed the world, and there are conversations that change *your* world.

ICONS TO GUIDE YOU

You'll find icons scattered throughout the book to guide you to particular features and focus on important bits.

This icon offers the opportunity to reflect upon an important point in the text. It often captures the essence of what I've been discussing in a particular section.

This icon invites you to watch out for particular traps or difficulties in conversation. Heed these and you'll make great progress!

This icon suggests activities for you to try in order to hone your conversational skills. Conversation is a practical pursuit and you'll get the most out of the book by having a go, without worrying too much about getting things right the first time you try them.

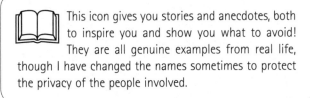
This icon gives you stories and anecdotes, both to inspire you and show you what to avoid! They are all genuine examples from real life, though I have changed the names sometimes to protect the privacy of the people involved.

So now you're ready to go. Read the book from cover to cover, or dip in and out of different sections – whatever suits you best.

Of course I can't pin down the full range of glorious, moving, world-changing, creative, exciting, sexy, gentle, compassionate, kind and moving conversations over the globe. But even to explore a little our communication with each other opens up a chink on a world that deserves our close attention. Enjoy the book, and happy talking!

> "Speech is civilization itself. The word, even the most contradictory word, preserves contact – it is silence which isolates."
> – Thomas Mann, *The Magic Mountain*

Part One

Introducing Conversation

THE DANCE OF CONVERSATION

"Conversationally, we were Fred and Ginger – spin, slide, shuffle, bend."
– Marisa de los Santos

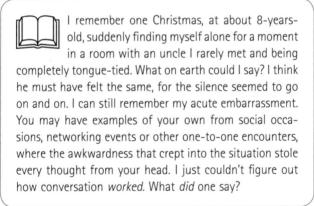 I remember one Christmas, at about 8-years-old, suddenly finding myself alone for a moment in a room with an uncle I rarely met and being completely tongue-tied. What on earth could I say? I think he must have felt the same, for the silence seemed to go on and on. I can still remember my acute embarrassment. You may have examples of your own from social occasions, networking events or other one-to-one encounters, where the awkwardness that crept into the situation stole every thought from your head. I just couldn't figure out how conversation *worked*. What *did* one say?

1.1   A dance for two

Conversation is clearly about talking, but talking doesn't make a conversation. George Bernard Shaw once commented to a young lady that she had lost the art of conversation but not, unfortunately, the power of speech! If everyone talks incessantly without listening to anyone else, there's no conversation. It's just people talking one after another or, more often, one over another. You've probably found yourself in a group at some time where everyone's busy expressing opinions and no one's listening to anyone else. It isn't a very satisfying experience.

The word "conversation" is made up of *con*, "with" and *versare*, "turn". Conversation is turn and turn about – you alternate.

Conversation is all about taking turns. It's a dialogue, not a monologue. You share the talking time; you also listen and acknowledge.

One person may talk more than another, just as in a dance one person may perform more complicated steps than another, but there's equality in conversation. It's very hard to have a good conversation with someone who intimidates or patronizes you or with someone who is intimidated *by* you.

The to and fro of a good conversation feels easy and natural, with both parties taking part and responding spontaneously to each other. Mme de Staël, a great French conversationalist of the eighteenth century, described conversation as a means of "reciprocally and rapidly giving one another pleasure; of speaking just as quickly as one thinks; of spontaneously enjoying one's self".

In the dance of conversation, both players take part in the steps of the dance with their thoughts, feelings and body language. You don't shut down your listening to think of what to say next or to make unspoken comments internally. The dance doesn't stop. The art is as much in drawing out the other person as in airing your own thoughts and opinions. There's mutual respect for each other – I'm okay, you're okay. In most conversations you don't make it deliberately difficult for the other person to dance their steps – you facilitate their moves, even when they appear clumsy.

When musicians and actors want to describe a particularly satisfying performance, they often call it a "conversation" to describe the feeling of connection that travels both ways. "My stand-up is quite good now – it's just like a big conversation each time", says the comedian Eddie Izzard. "A good quartet is like a good conversation among friends interacting to each other's ideas", suggests the saxophonist Stan Getz. "When I play live, it's a conversation that we're all having with the song", says the singer–songwriter Tori Amos.

A SUBTLE HUMAN ART

Like music, good conversation is a subtle art. When you converse with someone, you are doing many things simultaneously. You are listening to what the other person has to say, while picking up the nuances of voice tone and the clues in their appearance and body language, and at the same time you are in a state of readiness to respond easily and naturally with words of your own. No wonder doing it well takes practice!

In 1950, the computer scientist Alan Turing tested to what extent computers could learn how to converse naturally. He published a paper on artificial intelligence, *Computing Machinery and Intelligence*, in which he described a test where a subject attempts to have a conversation with a computer. The computer would be said to "think" if its responses in conversation resembled those of a real human being. Anyone who tries the test finds it doesn't take more than a few words before you know it's a machine!

Here is a transcription of a test conversation I had with the computer. The computer is called Eliza, and "she" begins the conversation.

ELIZA: Is something troubling you?
ME: *Well, yes it is.*
ELIZA: You seem to be quite positive.
ME: *Not at all. I've just said something is troubling me.*
ELIZA: That's quite interesting.
ME: *Well, do you want to hear what it is?*
ELIZA: You're not really talking about me – are you?
ME: *No, I'm trying to tell you about my troubles if you'll just listen!*
ELIZA: Why "no"?
ME: (reacting in frustration, even though I knew it was a machine!) *Oh, you just don't get it!*

The sentences individually sound plausible, but the conversation as a whole doesn't make sense. It's easy to detect that it's not two live people. Human conversation is indeed complex and harder to replicate than we might imagine.

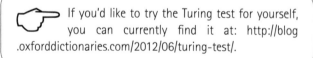 If you'd like to try the Turing test for yourself, you can currently find it at: http://blog .oxforddictionaries.com/2012/06/turing-test/.

1.2 The traditional "conversationalist"

Much advice on conversation takes little heed of this subtle dance for two. Almost all books on the art of conversation from the twentieth century and earlier, emphasize the need to be articulate and witty, and have interesting things to say on any subject. Apart from general advice to be pleasant and courteous, they mostly ignore the complex dance of connection.

It's good to remember that conversation was important for entertainment and education in the era before radio, television, the Internet and the rest, as this helps to explain the emphasis on content and performance. In the eighteenth century, conversation in the French salons was an indispensable entertainment – a cultivated and artificial art with fixed rules. Here wit, rhetoric, gallantry, flattery, teasing, joking and irony all played an important part. People learned how to perform with style. A great conversationalist was described as one who could hold the attention of everyone. In the nineteenth century, Thomas de Quincey wrote with admiration that Samuel Coleridge swept the stage with his articulate performance. The experience of spending an evening in the company of the great man was like witnessing a great unstoppable river. The poet "swept at once into a continuous strain of dissertation, certainly the most novel, the most finely illustrated, and traversing the most spacious fields of thought, by transitions the most just and logical, that it was possible to conceive".

The twentieth-century philosopher Sir Isaiah Berlin was called the greatest conversationalist who had ever lived because he was able to perform on any theme with wonderful dexterity, "soaring through every imaginable subject, spinning, flipping, hanging by his heels and without a touch of showmanship". The novelist Virginia Woolf had a similar ability to spin off during conversation into fantastic flights of fancy, while everyone else stopped speaking and just sat around in admiration. Churchill was another magnificent talker of the twentieth century, with a lesser reputation as a listener.

The "art of conversation" is still taught with similar emphasis in some private seats of learning, not as a meeting of minds, but as a tour de force. Thus we get many public figures and pillars of the establishment who are excellent at performing but less good at tuning-in. This interpretation of conversation is also perpetuated today in television panel games where each panel member tries to outdo the others in wit, entertainment and erudition. One example is the British television show *QI*, which appears to promote educated conversation, but in reality serves as a vehicle for bravura performances of erudition and wit – most notably those of host Stephen Fry.

> Remember, the art of conversation is *not* the same as the art of talking. Wit, eloquence and knowledge are one thing. Conversational skill is something more.

In these times of mass communication, brilliance of oratory is not enough. You can't be a great conversationalist on your own. It's always a dance for two or more, consisting of talking and listening, listening and talking.

CICERO'S SUMMARY

The earliest commentators on conversation grasped this two-way dance. The Roman writer Cicero, one of the earliest writers on the art of conversation, offers practical and timeless advice:

1. Take turns in speaking.
2. Speak clearly and easily but not too much!
3. Do not interrupt the other person.
4. Be courteous.
5. Deal seriously with serious matters and gracefully with lighter ones.
6. Never criticize people behind their backs.
7. Stick to subjects of interest to both or all of you.
8. Don't talk about yourself.
9. Never lose your temper.

It's a useful list as you start to think about how to make conversation work for you . . . though I think some of us today would struggle with number 8. Maybe we could put instead, "Don't talk about yourself *all* the time!"

1.3 What's conversation for?

 I'd like to ask you two questions before we continue:

- What do you think a conversation is for?
- What makes a conversation good, enjoyable or satisfying for you?

Jot down your answers before you continue reading.

One frequent answer to these questions is that conversation is about gaining information – for example, finding out interesting facts or learning new things – or getting a result. In other words, the *content* – what you actually talk *about* – is the most important thing. People who give this answer usually enjoy information and ideas, and get satisfaction out of exchange of opinions and debate.

They think of conversation as the *means to an end*. You might notice that many specialized conversations, and ordinary conversations too, are about getting something for yourself – finding out something you don't know, exchanging information, gaining new business, negotiating to get a sale, influencing people to take up your ideas, motivating them to follow your lead, and so on. (These are the subjects of many self-help books!)

Other people answer differently. They hold that conversation is about getting to know people, making friends, building relationships, understanding each other better or enjoying people's company. In other words, the *connection* between the two people is what matters most. They enjoy the feeling of getting closer to another human being, of sharing and building rapport, and enjoying each other's company. The content of a conversation takes second place to the feelings of connection, the tone and atmosphere of the discussion, and the sense of a growing friendship.

Your view of the purpose of the exchange considerably influences your approach to conversation. Look at the answers you jotted down. Do you find they point more to *content* and *result* or to *connection?*

Successful conversations are about both content and connection in varying proportions. But connection is always key. Even if you are focused on a particular outcome from a conversation, it will go better if you pay attention to connecting with the other person as well as to getting what you want from the exchange. Connection is often the means by which you achieve a desired outcome, but can also stand on its own as the sole purpose of an exchange.

Your first and important step, in starting up a conversation with someone, is to make connection. So how do you do that? That's the subject of the next chapter.

2

CONNECTING IS WHAT MATTERS MOST

"The reason you don't understand me Edith, is that I'm talkin' to you in English and you're listening in dingbat!"
– US TV character, Archie Bunker

Connection does indeed matter. It's the means of creating a link with another person at the start of a conversation, and it's the lubricant that keeps it flowing. It's how people understand each other's meaning, an essential if you wish to influence anyone. It's the road to friendship, closeness and intimacy, irrespective of what you're talking about.

 Good connection creates the necessary trust for a satisfying conversation.

You can usually tell when two people in conversation are connecting well. If you are close enough to hear what they are saying, you discover that they've found a subject that engages them both. If you can't hear the actual words, you can still detect a musical to-and-fro rhythm and similar tones of voice. Even if you are completely out of earshot, you can visually catch a flowing dance between the two people as they mirror each other's physiology and move in harmony with each other.

 UK Prime Minister Margaret Thatcher once spoke optimistically about the new president of the USSR: "I like Mr Gorbachev. We can do business together." If you view news clips of their meetings, you can observe that they feel comfortable in each other's company. From that sense of connection they were able to have positive and productive conversations about relations between their two countries.

Many conversations lack this vital ingredient. To clarify what connection is and isn't, and what gets in the way of connection, I want to give you several examples of conversations where it *doesn't* happen. I think you're going to recognize several of them!

2.1 Conversational drains

When a conversation is just two people talking without connection, the experience can be far from pleasurable. I'm sure you have suffered frustrating or boring conversations in your life – maybe you still do!

Oprah Winfrey was once asked what she wished she had known earlier in her life. She replied that she would like to have been able to distinguish between "radiators" and "drains". She explained that "radiators" are people who give out something positive, such as warmth and kindness or energy and enthusiasm. "Drains" on the other hand are people who are negative and self-critical and suck the energy out of you.

You're probably familiar with what she was talking about. After chatting with some people, you walk away with a spring in your step feeling energized and inspired. Other people exhaust you. After a conversation with them you retreat feeling that all your energy has been sapped and nothing has been given in return.

Who are the drains in your life and what makes them draining? You may find some of them here.

ENTHUSO-BORE

The Enthuso-bore exudes energy and enthusiasm. But enthusiasm can be extremely tiring for others when it's self-centred and one-sided, without any acknowledgement of the needs of the listener.

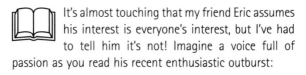 It's almost touching that my friend Eric assumes his interest is everyone's interest, but I've had to tell him it's not! Imagine a voice full of passion as you read his recent enthusiastic outburst:

"Well, I must tell you! I've been looking for the DL53 NBQ ancillary for my Turbo P59 for the past 13 months, and I've just found it! Of course, even though it's the correct model it doesn't quite fit the 2013 machine and I'm going to have to tweak it a bit. It's devilishly tricky to fit – they don't make those machines to be repaired do they? I had to buy a special 2LCU adjuster – and that's not a run-of-the-mill size I can tell you! I eventually ran one down in a workshop in Crouch End that source their widgets from the Ukraine – quite extraordinary . . . They were excellent – the only people who understood the problem, and knew what I was talking about . . . "

Well, I'm glad someone did!

 If you never take breath or use your eyes to check whether your listeners are following you intellectually and emotionally, they'll quickly lose interest.

Sometimes the context is emotional, and the speaker so bound up in their romantic bubble that they fail to notice a lack of response. Mattie is so in love, she has to tell her friend *everything*:

> "Well, I decided to wear my white skirt – you know, the one with buttons down the side – 'cos he hasn't seen it before. And I did my hair that way you said suited me best, straightened and brushed to the side. And as soon as he saw me he said how great I was looking, and took my hand. Well, actually, first he just paused and looked at me for a moment – I thought I'd die! – it was such an intense look, and he almost smiled – you know when a man smiles but it's not quite a smile, but it sort of is . . . and then he took my hand, and said he wanted to take me to dinner. But first . . . oh, wait a minute, yes, he said then that he thought we were going to have a great evening together, and then . . . – I'm not boring you am I? – then we got a cab – well he got the cab, and whisked me off to this amazing restaurant and the dinner, oh the dinner, you'll never guess . . ."

Poor friend! On other occasions, there's an unspoken competition to speak more and louder than anyone else. Young people's author Megan McCafferty remembers being overcome with a feeling of exhaustion at college parties, where each person wanted to be the smartest, funniest person in the room, and everyone talked over everyone else, interrupting and pushing themselves forward to prove that they were indeed the smartest, funniest person in the world.

Enthusiasm on its own is no guarantee of a good conversation.

ROBO-CHORE

Robo-chore speakers are like Enthuso-bores without the enthusiasm. They don't want to be in conversation with you at all, but feel an obligation. Spend five minutes with a Robo-chore and you are longing for even an Enthuso-bore! They treat conversation as a tedious chore. Even as they expound on the advantages of self-catering in Greece or the best lawnmower for a sloping lawn, they are not finding the subject the least bit interesting themselves and are not really bothered whether you are or not. They are just doing what you "have" to do in certain social situations – make conversation for the sake of politeness without having anything engaging to say. And they are not interested in listening to you either, so no connection can be made. Under those circumstances, many people just count their losses and go through the motions.

If you don't want to proceed in that way, you may want to gently challenge the person to be more real by asking genuine questions, and refusing to be satisfied with stock answers.

> **!O** If you prepare topics and current information to take to networking and social events, beware! Make sure that you find your subjects interesting yourself, and watch out for signs of interest or boredom in the other person.

ECHO-BORE

The Echo-bore takes no risks, introduces not one single idea, opinion or feeling, but just agrees with you, repeats your words or says what's most obvious, so that you are forced to do all the running and don't get anything in return. This behaviour can stem from nervousness, and if you are able put the person at ease, there is a chance that you can move on to a better conversation. But if you get stuck at this repetitive stage, the Echo-bore remains unknowable, and neither party gets any value from a conversation:

>   I just love Mozart don't you?
> E-B *Oh yes, Mozart . . . lovely.*
>   Which symphony is your favourite?
> E-B *Well, I love them all you know, it's very . . .*
>   Mine's the 40th.
> E-B *Yes, yes, that's the best, isn't it? Yes, that's the favourite, yes . . .*
>   It's the way he captures sadness even in a major key.
> E-B *Yes, that's right, yes. It's really sad music, isn't it?*

Comedians Mel Smith and Griff Rhys Jones played creatively on this idea of lopsided conversations in a series of amusing sketches in their UK comedy show, *Alas Smith and Jones.* Smith was the acknowledged expert of the pair, and Jones the gormless

Echo-bore. You can find various clips of their sketches on YouTube, for example: youtube.com/watch?v=Ok_42shL_5E.

> You may wish to be pleasing as a conversationalist, but if you risk nothing, you get nothing.

THE EGO-BORE

"He was like a cock who thought the sun had risen to hear him crow", remarks sharp Mrs Poyser about a gentleman in George Eliot's *Adam Bede*. Some people have an uncanny narcissistic ability to steer any conversation towards themselves.

Ego-bores are like Enthuso-bores, but with a single exclusive subject – themselves. For Ego-bores, their partners in conversation exist only to shine a light on them. If you introduce a subject they will seize control of it at once, for example:

>> I couldn't see you last week as I had to rush down to my mother in Brighton because she's seriously ill, so I . . .

> Ego-B: *I love Brighton. It's my place. I go there all the time. There's a little restaurant there where I'm treated like family; they know me so well that they even offer me delicacies not on the menu.*

>> Oh, right. Yes, it's a lovely town for restaurants – my mother's lived there for years. We used to love meandering down the Lanes and . . .

> Ego-B: *I don't touch the Lanes – they're touristy, and so passé. I get everything on the Internet these days, doesn't everyone? I'm a genius at it actually. Amazing some of the bargains I've managed! Did I tell you about the*

> *time I bought a solid gold watch for £10? Sheer brilliance! Well, I ...*

Count the frequency of "I", "me" and "my"! Such conversationalists are too know-all, too patronizing and too "windbag" to give pleasure to anyone else. Ego-bores probably won't be aware of the impact of their behaviour unless you are fairly robust and seize the conversation yourself or challenge their comments directly.

QUEEN OF GOSSIP

The Queen of Gossip is very happy to engage in conversation, as long as she (or he of course) can speak negatively about other people. Initially, the shared confidences of gossip can feel bonding, particularly if you secretly agree with the other person's opinion. There's nothing like mutual dislike and a set of grievances to create consensus! But afterwards you're left with an unpleasant sour taste, and the uneasy suspicion that you may become their next victim! So trust is absent, and there's no true connection.

 Beware any feeling of connection when you gossip; it's skin deep. One of the great arts of conversation is to leave certain things unsaid at the most tempting moment!

MOANING MICKEY AND MINNIE

Finally, Moaning Mickeys and Minnies are happy to converse, but take such a negative attitude to life that they drag you down and exhaust you. If you are tempted to help make things better or find solutions to their woes, you soon find that they are not looking for solace – they want a listener to fan the flames, not put them out.

MM: *Awful weather isn't it? Don't you hate snow?*
Yes, it's pretty cold. Makes you long for summer . . .

MM: *Mind you, I can't stand the heat – it's really bad for my breathing.*
Well, yes, it can get too hot sometimes . . .

MM: *It's never one thing but it's the other. Once this lot thaws it'll be rain for a month, I'm telling you, really bad for my rheumatism . . .*
I'm sorry to hear that you . . .

MM: *Yes, it's really bad. But I blame the government – right bad lot all of them!*
Right . . .

Some moaners can rant for England and the other person never gets a word in at all:

"As I said to him, I said, like, it's not as if we go on holiday very often with you working and everything and it'd only be for a week and I deserve a break and he's like, well someone has to earn the money round here and I'm like, well that's rich with you out of work as much as in, and who's going to look after the children if I don't, and he's like, you always bring up that old excuse, and they're at school all day so it's not as if they're round your ankles, and I'm like, excuse me! – who does all the shopping and cooking and cleaning and if that isn't a job I don't know what is, and I mean, he's just out of order, don't you agree? . . ."

I think the first breath comes around about here!

Moaners love to dump their stuff on you. They tell you all about their troubles at length and in detail. Then they cheerfully tell you they've enjoyed the chat and walk off. Meanwhile, without having said a word yourself, you are left swamped under a truckload of negativity! Instead of their long spiel, they could have said, "I have this great weight of bad stuff – carry it around for me, could you?"

Moaning is sometimes called the English national pastime. People grouse and grumble, they whine and carp, they gripe and grouch, they bitch and beef, they kvetch and whinge, they belly-ache and complain. When people are thrown together on TV reality shows, such as *Big Brother* and *I'm A Celebrity, Get Me Out Of Here*, moaning – together with gossip – becomes a popular activity. But don't be deceived that mutual moaning is a conversation – the participants don't really connect.

> Moaning Mickies and Minnies usually warm to their task like a tanker getting up speed, so it's wise to nip their spiel in the bud and move the conversation onto more positive topics as soon as you can.

So how are the "radiators" different from "drains"? We're going to explore various elements as we proceed, but perhaps the most fundamental is that radiators understand the two-way character of conversation. They know how to *connect*.

2.2 Finding common ground

What is the magic ingredient of connection? You connect when there's a flow or rhythm between you. Like a pendulum it can swing fast or slow, but there's a rhythm and a pattern. You don't find a pendulum swinging slowly in one direction and then suddenly coming back fast. One swing resembles the previous one, and as the rhythm changes, both sides are influenced.

Building a connection with another person is about creating rhythm – or similarity. And the most obvious, though certainly not the only, way to do that is to find a common subject. By common, I mean "in common", but also "common" – everyday and general.

Introduce an easy everyday subject like travel, home or recreation that the other person will find easy to add to. You're not very likely to find a connection if you ask, "I'm a great fan of corkscrews. Have you seen the *Corkscrews of the World Magazine* this month?" or "I understand that the sport of Dwarf Throwing is really taking off in Western Australia. Exciting, isn't it?" The purpose is to create a connection, not show off your specialist knowledge, so keep it simple and general, and be willing to shift around till you find a mutual subject.

 Picture this scenario. Two people meet at a wedding:

How do you know the bride or groom?
I used to clean Mary's flat.
Oh, right. I'm Jeremy's boss at Boult, Chase and Flatten International. Do you live near here?

> *I live just the other side of Birmingham in Shard End.*
> *You?*
>
> Well, actually, we've just flown in from the Maldives
>   – we own an island there. Do you know the
>   archipelago?
>
> *No, we usually go to Burgundy on holiday.*
>
> Oh, France, my favourite country in the world – we
>   often go to the south of France. The food . . . !
>
> *The cheeses are great, aren't they?*
>
> Oh, French cheeses! I think they're the best in the
>   world! Have you tried Epoisses? – That smell!

And after a rocky start, they are off, with a sense of relief
at having found a subject that interests them both.

The conversation will go well if they share their experiences by taking an interest in each other's comments. So,
after exploring cheeses, the boss might well decide to stick
with his companion's experience of Burgundy for a while
before telling his own story of the south of France. For
instance:

> So you go to Burgundy? There's a great canal system
>   there I believe, isn't there? Do you know it?

FAVOURITE OBJECTS OF ATTENTION

As you take those first tentative steps in conversation, look out
for people's preferred focus of attention. Whatever the subject
under discussion, people like to home in on particular elements,
and their preferences tend to be fairly consistent.

Think about your own preferences. Which of the following types of question interest you most?

Information – facts, numbers and statistics
- How does this year's growth compare with last?
- What percentage of the population owns a car?

Technical talk – "widgets"
- What new features does your camera have?
- How does that app work?

People and gossip
- Do you know why David left the company in a hurry?
- Guess what she said to her boss?

Feelings
- How did Sophie cope with moving so many times?
- How do you feel about the change of leadership?

Abstract concepts, ideas
- Do you think there can there be peace without equality?
- Don't you find it extraordinary that we can now visualize the activity of the brain in real time?

Time and place – where, when
- Whereabouts were you in India?
- When will you take your final exams?

If you listen closely to what people say and the questions they ask you'll soon notice their preferences, and that gives you a good idea of how to engage them further and put them at ease. You don't have to stay with their preferences forever of course!

2.3   Finding a common language

We all have particular words and phrases we use more often than others. Professions have particular jargons and groups of friends have common turns of phrase. If you just imitate someone's language you'll sound like a parrot, but you can tune into certain characteristics of the other person's language to connect better.

Some people, particularly in a work context, use a large number of abstract terms that lend formality to their speech. Here's a typical example from a business conference:

> The issue of smooth communication channels between our operations is of great importance. Given the lack of regulation of this market and the huge daily turnover, the need to have a well-functioning framework of communication and cooperation cannot be underestimated.

Issue, communication, operations, importance, regulation, market, turnover, framework, cooperation – they are all abstract terms that you can neither see, hear, touch, taste or smell, and they provide a business shorthand for discussion without specifics. In some contexts you'll find people feel more at home if you introduce the more formal "issue of communication" rather than asking, "So how best are we going to talk to each other and keep in touch?"

Compare such abstract language with the more everyday colourful language of the senses where you see, hear and feel what is being said. Sense Martin Luther King's "desert state, sweltering with the heat of injustice" and his description of a world where he hears "freedom ring from the prodigious hilltops" to the "snowcapped Rockies" in his famous "I have dream" speech. Sense Winston Churchill's great British fleet – "gigantic castles of steel wending their way across the misty, shining sea, like giants bowed in anxious thought".

People feel you are on their wavelength if you use a similar *kind* of language. Moreover, different people use one sense more than another, and it tends to show up in their language. So one person says, "I *see* what you mean", while another says, "that *sounds* like good sense", and a third remarks, "I *get* it". If you then respond using similar visual, auditory or feeling language, they naturally feel comfortable with you.

 Patsy presented a problem in coaching, and said:

"He's pretty depressed at the moment. I can't quite put my finger on it, but he's struggling to get up in the morning, says he feels strange, and when I try to grasp what he's saying, he just sinks further down in the bed and I feel he's avoiding the issue."

Her words were full of feeling/moving language. If I'd responded in visual language, "I *see* your problem. Do you want my *perspective* on it?" I think she would have felt misunderstood. Instead I answered her in similar feeling language. "That's *rough.* So you want to *get to the heart* of what's *going on?*"

2.4 Non-verbal connection

Content is the most obvious feature of conversation, and as we've seen, you can build connection through finding a common theme and language. But connection happens most strongly beneath the surface, in the non-verbal aspects of communication.

 You get on someone's wavelength most easily and surely by tuning in to the sound of their voice and their body language.

BODY LANGUAGE

When people are connecting well they tend to share similar movements or lack of movement. If the speaker is leaning forward and talking passionately about something, the listener is likely to be leaning forward too to connect with the passion. If the speaker is gesticulating energetically, maybe the listener is nodding energetically too. Thus you find that the body language of the listener mirrors that of the speaker, or at least echoes the movement in a complementary movement.

If you are in tune with someone this happens naturally. When you first meet someone, you can help this natural process along by consciously fitting your body language to theirs. If they keep still as they speak, they'll feel at ease with you if you are fairly still too. If they gesture a lot, they'll feel more heard if you are fairly mobile too.

Body language is often obvious; when people wave their arms around you don't miss it! But there's subtlety too. Look out for the following when you're having a conversation:

- Is the speaker's body relaxed or taut?
- How often do they look at you?
- Is their posture relaxed and open or tight and closed?
- To what extent does their skin colour change as they talk about something?
- How fast or slow is their breathing?
- How deeply do they breathe?

If you take on their way of standing, moving, looking and being, you enter more and more into their world, and as you do that you begin to understand them better too.

Watch out! No one wants to be imitated as if you're making fun of them! Observe people mirroring each other naturally when they're on a similar wavelength. Then when you match someone deliberately you can do it in a similar, unobtrusive way.

A participant on one of my courses who tried this experiment was stunned after taking on her course partner's way of being for several minutes. "So *this* is what it's like to be you," she exclaimed. "I had no idea!" She reported feeling more cramped and constrained – as if she were deliberately holding herself together – and said it made her feel more wary and anxious. This information enabled her to understand the other person better. There are many ways of being in the world.

VOICE TONE

Tuning in applies to sound as well. If you listen to the qualities of a speaker's voice and moderate your own voice to make it more similar to theirs, they are likely to feel more heard and understood. Again, this happens naturally when one person empathizes with another. If a friend of yours speaks of unhappiness in a low voice, it's very likely that you naturally reply in a low quiet voice to demonstrate empathy and understanding:

> (Low despairing voice) I lost my job – after 20 years in the same place. I don't know what to do.
> (Low empathetic voice) *That's so rough – times are hard at the moment, aren't they?*

It works with high energy too:

> (In great excitement) I won the trip to Fiji! Two weeks in the best hotel, all expenses paid!
> (High enthusiastic tone) *That's fantastic! Wow, a free exotic holiday – you must be thrilled!*

Thus the speaker feels that the responder shares her excitement. You can imagine the negative effect if the listener in the second example were to respond in a low disgruntled tone:

> Huh. Some people have all the luck. I've never won anything in my life, and not likely to either.

Just as with body language, the more you can tune in to the subtleties of the speaker's voice, the easier you will find it to connect with them.

 Experiment with different aspects of voice:

- Speed – faster or slower
- Volume – louder or quieter
- Pitch – higher or lower
- Range – wide or narrow pitch range

Often, adjusting even one of these aspects brings you closer to the other person – for example, slowing down to talk to someone elderly, or speaking in a deeper voice to someone authoritative.

2.5   Energetic connection

"Connection is why we're here."
– Brene Brown

Connection happens most strongly at a level beyond what you see and hear. You might call it a harmonizing of internal energy. The speaker may move around a lot and you may not, but if you respond internally to the energetic sense of their movement, you'll connect with their energy even without visible movement. Finding a meeting place energetically is much more powerful that spotting a subject matter in common – and subtler too.

To practise connecting via non-verbal communication, choose a time when you are in casual conversation with someone.

First observe the other person's body language and listen to the variations in their voice tone, with the intention of entering into their world. Listen of course to what they have to say as well. Be especially aware of their breathing, which corresponds closely to their energy.

Then join in their dance, responding to their movement and sounds. You will sense the energy flowing to and fro naturally between you. Then gradually, you will begin to feel their underlying energy and understand better who they really are. Once you have connected energetically with the other person, then either of you can lead smoothly to a different energy. You don't need to stay stuck in the same energetic space forever!

> **!** Note that matching energy is not the same as copying a mood. For example, when I respond to an angry person whose energy is high and strong, I match their energy and speak my first few words strongly too so that they know I am tuning in to their mood. But I am not speaking angrily myself. I match the energy, not the mood.

When two people in conversation are on the same wavelength, they are literally so. An article in *Frontiers in Auditory Cognitive Neuroscience* quotes research from Gothenburg University in Sweden, which demonstrates that choir singers synchronize their heartbeats as they sing together. Such entrainment can also be found when women who live together evolve synchronous menstrual cycles, or pendulum clocks in proximity to each other gradually come into synchronicity. Energetic connection is a powerful force.

When people find an energetic rhythm in common as they speak with each other, they naturally feel comfortable and in tune. As you practise this skill, it helps to have the intention of entering the other person's world with curiosity, respect and acknowledgement.

 Your intention is more powerful than any physical matching of body language or voice.

2.6 Flexibility

When you adjust to someone else's wavelength by matching their energy, they are calling the tune, not you, so it can feel as if you are handing over your power to them. When I introduced this concept to an executive in a coaching session he complained that it felt weak. "If I want my staff to respect me, I need to be strong and consistent", he said.

We went on to explore the concept of strong and consistent *values* and flexible *behaviour*. I gave him the metaphor of a tree. A rigid tree falls down very easily in wind. A live tree that has strong life flowing through it from root to leaf shows its strength in moving with the wind rather than in resisting. There is a respect in flowing with the energy of another person that invites respect in return, and allows you to feel the moving life of the interchange.

If you want an interesting conversation with the potential for a positive outcome, you need flexibility. If one person is in a rigid role – even a "good" role such as "strong and consistent" for example – then the other person gets stuck in an unchanging role too. Even when a "superior" is speaking with a "subordinate", the conversation works best when there's a feeling of mutual respect and equality that allows movement and flow.

GOING WITH THE FLOW

Once you are in harmony with each other through your flexibility, you can smoothly influence the conversation and lead your partner in a particular direction. It's all about going with the flow and influencing within flow.

The US mathematics professor Michael Starbird gives a great example of teaching with flow. He deals with a student's mistakes without once interrupting the flow with a criticism or negative comment, but instead agrees with her and leads her on from there.

"I don't want to say the answer because I know it's wrong," says the student.

"I'm sure you're correct that it's wrong," he replies. "But tell me anyway."

She tells him and it's wrong.

"Congratulations for knowing it was wrong!" says the tutor. "Tell me one thing that's wrong with it."

She tells him.

"Then tell me how you might fix that defect," he asks her.

She's able to do this too.

"Is it right now?" he asks.

"No," she replies.

"You're absolutely correct again," he says. "It is wrong."

And so the dialogue continues towards a positive conclusion, with the student still in good spirits. The professor flows with the student, but is also leading.

It's harder to go with the flow if you're in a meeting where everyone is talking at once, particularly if you are someone who likes to reflect before you speak. You may have found in the past at meetings that by the time you have framed your intervention you've already missed your moment. In that case, the first words of your interruption need to be as fast and loud as the general melée: you might use an introductory phrase to interrupt, such as "*I'd* like to add something here". Once your interruption has been heard, you can make your point, gradually adjusting to your normal volume and pace, and people will listen.

 The ability to join the flow and then steer it to your own pace is a valuable conversational skill. You match, then you lead.

BREAKING CONNECTION

Flexibility helps to build connection. It also enables you to break connection when you need to move on.

Elise worked with clients who were often troubled and anxious, and she was a born listener, empathetic and sensitive to their needs. The trouble was, she was such a good listener that clients would keep her on the phone for hours at a time, simply because she was so in-tune that the sympathetic connection was never broken. Elise became desperate. She felt she was holding the world's troubles on her shoulders and her time was spiralling out of control. She was so good at connecting she didn't know how to disconnect.

Seeking help, she discovered that it was mainly her sympathetic voice tone that kept her in tune with her clients, and so long as she continued to use this tone it was just impossible to bring the conversation to an end. So she learned to lighten her tone and speed up a little when she wanted to finish a conversation. Then her clients would gradually sense that the conversation was coming to an end and allowed her to conclude gracefully. She found that standing up and walking around also helped her to change to a more lively state.

When you're ready to move on from a conversation, try any or all of the following:

- Change your voice tone. A higher quicker tone usually works well.
- Stand up – even if the other person can't see you – as this changes your energy.
- Summarize the conversation, if you like, to wrap it up.
- Tell the other person what you are going to do as a result of the conversation, if that helps to round it off.

For example:

(In an empathetic voice) It's certainly been a troubled few months for you.

(In a brighter voice) I hope the next few months are less eventful.

(Speeding up) It's been really good to talk to you. I look forward to hearing better news when I see you next.

(Very brightly) All the very best. Speak to you again soon. Goodbye.

DEALING WITH "DRAINS"

I started this chapter with a list of "drain" characters – so how would you connect with them? One way, using the concept of flexibility described here, would be to join their "game" and play by their rules to create connection. So if the speaker talks but doesn't ask questions, then you can take part in the conversation by interrupting to answer all the questions they haven't asked!

Surprisingly, a monologue speaker is often pleased when the listener becomes a talker too.

There is no need though to join in conversation that compromises your values. If you don't want to moan, gossip or engage in conversation that is boring for both of you, then let yourself off the hook. If a conversation is not going well, it isn't necessarily your fault. If you refuse to join the game on other people's terms, the energy of the conversation fizzles out, and they are unable to continue in the same vein. In breaking connection, you gain release.

Just a brief final word on connecting: it is true that you connect by stepping energetically into other people's shoes, to see the world from their point of view. However, it's important not to lose yourself in the process. Good honest conversation depends on you being fully present, and unafraid to be yourself. I come back to this important issue later.

3

GETTING IN THE RIGHT STATE

"Clearly she was expected to say something, but panic at having to speak stole the thoughts from her head."
– Shannon Hale, *The Goose Girl*

When a conversation is going well, you are absorbing a lot of information with a lively awareness of the other person and are busy thinking on your feet. Both of you are carrying on a silent conversation with yourself as well as a spoken one with the other person. This is fine and enjoyable if you're feeling at ease. If you are not feeling at ease, however, it's not so good. Techniques are useful and a good starting place for improving your conversational skills but they do not address most people's chief problem in holding a conversation – and that is tension, awkwardness, lack of ease or anxiety, all different aspects of *fear*. Such feelings can stop you thinking clearly, make you talk too much, cause you to dry up or make you sound self-conscious. So, in this chapter I look at an absolute essential for good conversation: the ability to be in a good state.

 More than skill, voice, fluency or intelligence, good conversation depends to an enormous extent on your state of mind.

Looking at lack of ease, an anxious state prevents you from seeing and hearing the other person properly; it floods your brain and prevents you from thinking clearly; it cuts you off from feelings of connection and isolates you in self-consciousness. T. S. Eliot's anxiety-ridden character, Prufrock, describes the situation accurately when he talks about having to "prepare a face to meet the faces that you meet", and of eyes that "fix you in a formulated phrase" and pin you "wriggling to a wall".

Social fear is very common. If you feel daunted by the idea of holding a conversation, you're in good company. In a US survey in the 1990s, 50% of the respondents considered themselves shy. Even world leaders and famous artists are not exempt. Nelson Mandela confessed that he never spoke up in meetings as a young man. "I was very nervous. I was really very nervous." Gandhi was so shy as a young lawyer that on one occasion he left the courtroom unable to speak. "Sometimes when I'm very nervous, I stutter," reported Marilyn Monroe in an interview.

You may not suffer from anything as extreme as this, or even use the word "fear" for your state of mind, but you may recognize some of the following at times when you speak with other people. See which apply to you:

- You feel self-conscious.
- You go into "performance" mode.
- You feel dull and uninteresting.
- You feel hyper and rush what you have to say.
- You find yourself "wittering on" and can't stop.
- You find you can't think of anything to say.
- The interaction feels stiff and artificial.

If you recognize any of these, you're going to find it useful to be able to influence your state of mind positively.

3.1 Managing your state

 Understand first that your state of mind does not have to be out of your control. It *is* possible to influence your state.

You are always in a state! It changes from moment to moment. Maybe you're driving while listening to music on a sunny day, feeling content. Suddenly, the traffic snarls up; you find yourself in a traffic jam and realize you're going to be late for your appointment. Your sunny mood evaporates and you become tense and anxious. Or you're struggling with a piece of work that doesn't seem to make sense and you look up from your desk to catch a warm smile from a favourite colleague. Your tension melts in an instant.

You can influence your state deliberately by changing your environment or your actions. You can calm yourself by listening to relaxing music, taking a warm scented bath or reading a novel. You might get into a more upbeat mood by dancing or watching an exciting film. You have a quiet evening before a big event the next day to put yourself in a focused state; you go for a walk to think through a tricky problem rather than trying to sort it out with phones ringing all around you. You recognize that particular tasks are easier in one state than another, so you don't attempt to make a life-changing decision after a sleepless night, or learn a new physical skill after drinking copious amounts of alcohol. It will vary from person to person, but certainly some states will be more productive for you than others in individual situations.

For conversation you want to find the inner state that allows you to tune in and listen well, think clearly, and have access to your feelings. And that means calming your fears and losing self-consciousness.

There are various ways to influence your inner state – I offer many tips and suggestions in my book *Butterflies and Sweaty Palms: 25 Sure-Fire Ways to Speak and Present with Confidence.* Here are some fundamental strategies:

BREATHE

Tension inhibits the breath, so remember to keep breathing! If you are about to enter a room for a social occasion, take a deep breath before you enter. When you speak, take a good breath as you open your mouth (it'll help your voice too). If you find yourself stuck and run out of something to say in a conversation, take a breath to move yourself on psychologically. Every time you take a good breath, you absorb calm and courage. The oxygen helps you to think clearly and find your words. Then every good out-breath is an opportunity to relax and find your sense of ease.

 Find a place where you can practise without being interrupted.

1. Stand or sit tall, shoulders and chest wide, the back of your neck relaxed, eyes soft, brow smooth. Fear often feels like a shutting down, so keep your body open and soft. Your skeleton stays upright and broad, and all your muscles melt and soften within that structure.

2. Now breathe out firmly with a "phoooo" sound, feel your body relax, and let fresh air fill up your lungs again without tension, letting the air enter

through your nose or mouth – or both. Repeat
this a couple of times more, taking your time.
3. Now breathe normally, and notice how your lungs
fill and empty much more fully when you are
relaxed.

Breathing is one of the most helpful things to remember
if you're feeling anxious. It comes to your rescue whether
you are just feeling a bit shy, or have reached a tense
critical moment in a conversation.

MOVE

When you feel awkward your first instinct may be to run away.
Then you hear a different inner voice urging you to "get a grip",
and you tense up to keep yourself on the spot. Giving yourself
permission to move counteracts this seizing up. You don't necessarily have to march up and down or wave your arms; it's just a
reminder to yourself that movement is allowed and helpful. Even
that simple reminder is probably enough to unlock your knees
and shoulders and jaw – and, most importantly, your *brain*. By
the way, breathing is movement in itself, so these two elements,
breathing and moving, go hand in hand.

Even if you are in a situation where others can observe you, you
can always move some part of your anatomy unobtrusively –
exercise your ankles and feet under the table, tighten your knees
and release again, squeeze your hands tightly together and then
relax them, and hollow your stomach, then release again.

Telling yourself to be calm is counter-productive if it makes you
tighten up. Movement of the body helps the activity of the mind.

You can be standing or sitting.

Try moving your body gently.

1. Slowly move your shoulders up and back and down.
2. Round your back and then arch it.
3. Move one hip forward then the other.
4. Raise your heels and point your feet alternately.
5. Shake your arms by your sides and feel your body wake up.
6. If you are standing, soften your knees and then walk up and down feeling open and relaxed.
7. If you want to be more energetic, jump up and down on the spot.

Think up your own movements to gently unstiffen all parts of your body – whatever is appropriate to your circumstances.

 Tense body = blocked mind. Relaxed body = free mind.

 Find a time and place where you can be undisturbed for 10 minutes or so.

1. Give yourself a random subject to talk about. Here are a few ideas: travel, the future, your country, life-changing events, friendship, money. You might like to write some subjects on small pieces of paper and then pick one at random.

2. Without further delay, start to walk up and down at a comfortable pace, and begin to talk out loud on your subject. If you don't know what you are going to say next, don't pause, but continue to walk until the next words come to you. Vary your pace by all means; but don't stop. Notice how the movement helps the words to come to you.

 Be aware that with movement, something to say will *always* come to you.

3.2 Collecting positive states

Your voice and physiology are affected by your state of mind, and your state of mind is affected by how you view your listeners. If you see them as potential adversaries or judges, you will be on your guard from the word go. If, on the other hand, you see them as friends and supporters, your attitude will be much more relaxed.

So your thoughts have a powerful influence on you. Whatever you think about and imagine changes your state. You can use this concept of imagination to access whatever state is going to be helpful to you.

What state of mind do you *want* to access in a conversation? I asked that question of someone I was coaching, and we had the following conversation:

> What state of mind do you want to access?
> *I'd like to enjoy it. I don't know if that is possible?*
> Enjoyment sounds good. What else?
> *I'd like to be able to trust that it's all going to be okay.*
> Great. Anything else?
> *I wish it could just happen without having to think too much about it – you know, like when a conversation just flows and everything seems easy.*

That gave us three states of mind to explore: enjoyment, trust and flow. So I asked him to collect some memories of all three.

We started with enjoyment. I asked him to remember vividly a specific time when he'd enjoyed himself, as if he were back in that time and place reliving the experience. He told me about a summer boat trip that he'd enjoyed and began to describe the trip enthusiastically. I reminded him that we were collecting states of mind – and suggested that he shut his eyes and put himself back in that occasion, and remember it with all his senses – the sights of the bright day and twinkling river, the sounds of splashing oars and happy voices, the smells of the river and the hot day, the feelings of warmth on the skin and the happy feeling in his body that brought a smile to his face. As he recalled the sensations of all his senses on that day, his breathing changed and his body relaxed. When he next spoke, his voice sounded calmer and deeper. "*Now* you know how to collect a state of mind," I said. "*That's* enjoyment."

It doesn't matter that the memory is not in the context of a conversation – it can be from any part of your life. It's about collecting a state of mind that produces particular feelings, thought patterns and physiology.

I used the same process with my client to recall other memories of enjoyment, and then to remember situations in which he had felt trust, and flow. He discovered that the more he exercised his sensual memory of good states, the easier it became to access them at will when he needed them.

 Think about a conversation you are going to have, or want to have, with someone:

1. Ask yourself the question: "What state of mind do I want to access for this particular conversation?"
2. Write down your answers. (e.g. confidence, calm, focus, enthusiasm, determination, relaxation, acceptance, trust etc.)
3. Take one of the states, and remember a specific time from any period and context of your life when you were in that state. Relive the

experience fully, seeing what you saw, hearing what you heard and feeling the emotions you felt at the time. Imprint the sensations into your muscle memory. Then find vivid memories for each of the other states. Learn "in your muscle" how they feel, so that you can access them again at will.

4. Run through in your mind the future conversation and bring to it the feelings, images, sounds and physiology of the states you have practised. Notice how your change in state impacts on the conversation. Even a slight shift in state changes the possibilities of the conversation considerably.

At some time in your life you have experienced every kind of state, mood and attitude. Through memory you have everything inside you that you need for each new situation. It's great to know that you are not at the mercy of your feelings and emotions, but can actually use them to help you when the going gets tough.

3.3 Staying present and aware

In conversation you want to be able to use your eyes to see, your ears to hear, and your body to feel – and then you can use this awareness to connect with the other person, and pick up all the hints and subtle clues in their conversation that allow you to respond appropriately.

If you feel self-conscious you are not doing that. You may be seeing, hearing and sensing, but in relation to yourself alone, not to the other person. You find that your sense of sight is occupied with pictures in your head – of previous occasions when you didn't know what to say, of negative visions of yourself that you imagine the other person is seeing or other unhappy scenarios. You find that your hearing is occupied in listening to your internal voice worrying, "Oh, what can I talk about? I've never met this person before, so I've no idea what subject to choose. This is so awkward, why on earth did I come?" And your valuable sense of feeling is flooded with how tense, shaky, worried and nervous you are feeling inside.

FOCUSING OUTSIDE YOURSELF

So how can you change this state of affairs? You can't stop thinking and sensing just by telling yourself not to. But you can shift your five senses from the inside to the outside. Either you can visualize images of disaster, listen to your internal dialogue and feel bad inside, or you can look with your eyes, listen to sounds in the environment and experience physical touch on the outside; you can't focus inside and outside at the same time. When internal thoughts threaten to sabotage you, external focus calms you and centres you in the present moment.

Make a deliberate intention to focus externally.

1. Look and notice something in your environment: the colour of the ceiling, the furniture, the pattern of the carpet or any other detail, and register consciously what you are looking at.
2. Now listen, and focus on the sounds outside your head – maybe the drone of central heating, traffic noise or people talking.
3. Now use the sense of feeling externally, by feeling your toes touching your shoes or your fingers touching each other.

As you focus externally and continue to breathe steadily, you find that your external senses expand their focus to pick up what the other person looks like and what they are saying. Then your sense of feeling is also able to engage in responding emotionally to the other person, enabling you to pick up nuances of their communication.

You don't have to think ahead about what to say next. When you are present in the moment, it emerges naturally out of listening. And when your senses are directed outward, you *are* present.

Though it may sound counter-intuitive, being present when you are fearful is partly about *allowing* yourself to be fearful, without self-judging. If you make great efforts to get things right – say the right things, put on the right expressions, not look nervous and so on – you will not only make mistakes just the same, you will also inhibit your natural flow. On the other hand, if you accept your vulnerability and allow yourself to be just the way you are, you find that any barriers between you and the other person dissolve. When you remain open and say what you are really thinking and feeling, other people feel they have permission to act similarly, and then the conversation becomes a genuine and satisfying one.

DEALING WITH SILENCE

You may find that you feel most anxious when there is silence. Many people have a danger alert signal that is set off by even minimal silence, triggering inner dialogue such as, "Oh, no one's talking! Help! This is awkward! Oh, what now?" At such moments, time plays tricks on you, and makes a couple of seconds feel like several minutes. If you observe people who are engaged happily in conversation, however, you notice that there are plenty of silences. There is silence while one person registers something interesting that the other person has said, and silence while they consider their response. There is a magical silence of connection, of mutual feeling and companionship. Often, the closer two people feel, the more comfortable they are with silence and the longer the pauses in a conversation.

A conversation thrives on moments of silence, and if you try to fill the space out of anxiety, you break the natural flow. Enjoy silence! It's as important as speech in conversation.

3.4 Curiosity

As you settle into yourself and feel more comfortable, and begin to notice the other person more, a wonderful new state emerges – you start to get curious. Curiosity is the golden facilitator of conversation because it creates questions, first in your head and then in a form that you can verbalize.

All children are curious. When did you stop getting curious? Maybe you never stopped? Certainly, as children we all knew unbounded curiosity. We asked question after question. We probably went through several months of repeating endlessly the single word, "Why?" But for many of us, something blocked our curiosity. Perhaps we were told that questions were intrusive or that the answers were not for us to know. Perhaps the whole business of "educating" us shut down that natural instinct. Perhaps we despaired of hearing true answers, felt we'd never understand or weren't good enough to deserve answers.

Well, you need curiosity for good conversation. So how do you awaken your curiosity?

Spend a little time reflecting on the following questions. You may like to have pen and paper at hand to record your answers, or get a friend to ask you the questions and record your answers for you. You may find you don't have answers immediately. Just sit for a minute and take your time to let the responses come to you. Get curious about curiosity!

- When do you allow yourself to be curious about another person?
- What gets in the way of your being curious?

- What state of mind allows you to be really curious?

When you have answered the questions, reflect on what the answers tell you about your relationship to curiosity. Curiosity isn't a means to make yourself look good, or a tool for putting the other person down, or a way to manipulate the other person without their noticing. It stems from a desire to enter the other person's world and get to know them better.

Genuine respectful curiosity creates connection and trust and opens the way to great conversations.

When you meet someone for the first time, or someone you don't know very well, respect will lead you wisely to start with questions that aren't too personal. A good guide is to get curious out loud about things you wouldn't mind people asking *you*. It's one thing to say, "Do you live in the neighbourhood?" It's another to ask, "Are you married, and if not why not?" The idea is to open pleasant avenues for the other person to chat informally, not to apply the Spanish Inquisition!

3.5 Trusting yourself and others

If you are sensitive to the other person, you can also be over-affected by their view of you, and spend your time worrying about their thoughts and reactions. Focus on the other person for sure, but don't lose *yourself*. In conversation two important fundamental assumptions support you.

- You are okay just the way you are. You are enough.
- Other people are to be trusted. You can think the best of other people and assume their best intentions.

If you believe these two assumptions, that belief will influence your state of mind and work positively for you.

You may resist the first point because it sounds as if you think you're perfect. Of course none of us is perfect – but it's okay to be yourself, without hiding behind some false image of perfection. It takes courage at times (and how!) not to hide behind a mask, but expressing your own feelings and your own opinions – with sensitivity – is the key to great relationships with others.

Assuming the best of others can sound naïve, but it's the route to genuine connection. When you assume the integrity and honour of others, that very assumption itself tends to attract those good qualities in other people.

GETTING A CONVERSATION GOING – THE BASICS

"It was one of those parties where you cough twice before you speak and then decide not to say it after all."
– P.G. Wodehouse

4.1   Breaking the silence

Often conversation just happens. You don't think about it and just discover yourself talking with someone, maybe responding to their questions and getting involved in some topic. In this chapter, I'm going to look at how you initiate a conversation, not one with an obvious aim and purpose, but a simple casual conversation with a stranger or someone you don't know well. For many people it's the hardest thing. How exactly *do* you initiate a casual conversation?

P.G. Woodhouse's famous character Bertie Wooster clearly struggled at times:

> *"What ho!" I said.*
> *"What ho!" said Motty.*
> *"What ho! What ho!"*
> *"What ho! What ho! What ho!"*
> *After that it seemed rather difficult to go on with the conversation.*
> *– (From My Man Jeeves)*

Someone has to be proactive if a conversation is to get off the ground. And it might as well be you – particularly as you're reading this book!

MAKE A COMMENT

Most casual conversations begin low key. You sow a seed without putting undue pressure on yourself and then you're easy about what might happen next. If a conversation gets going, that's great; if it doesn't, no matter. One way to sow the seed is to make a casual comment – just a simple remark into the air, easy to respond to or not, that doesn't put the other person on the spot or put them under an obligation to speak. For example, "What a cold day!" – yes, there's nothing wrong with the weather as an initial subject for conversation! – or, "Busy today . . . for a Monday."

Any simple casual comment is okay. A person standing by you can pick it up or not without embarrassment. If they don't, you've lost nothing. If they do, you've started the ball rolling. Use your eyes and ears to comment on things you notice, any simple off-the-cuff comment so long as it's not negative or intrusive.

☞ As you go about your daily life, collect comments that might spark a conversation. You can collect examples from remarks that you hear other people make and take a note of observations that you think of saying yourself.

Here are a few I heard this week:

Passing in the park: *"Good to be out now it's cooler, isn't it?"*

To the shop assistant: *"I like some of your new stock that's just come in . . ."*

To the pub assistant pouring a pint: *"It's a fantastic local beer, this."*

This is about focusing on the kind of things people say to strangers. You might hear something and think, "Well, I wouldn't say *that!*" Ask yourself why you wouldn't make such a comment. The exercise is about listening and reflecting. Make a note of comments that you like.

If you keep up with the news, you could choose to make a topical comment of general interest:

They've demolished the old supermarket in the High Street, I see.

I understand they arrested those bank robbers quite near here . . .

FLOAT IN A SIMPLE QUESTION

Another way to start a conversation is to ask a simple question. Again, take it easy, no pressure – it might get a conversation going, it might not.

In a queue: *"Been waiting long?"*
At the doctor's: *"Is this seat free?"*
At an event: *"Have you come far?"*

You might notice that these are "closed" questions – questions that can be answered monosyllabically with "yes" or "no" – and therefore are not guaranteed to get a conversation going. But in practice that is fine – being answerable with just yes or no, they are not intimidating, and serve the purpose of gently breaking the ice. You may get no reply or a brief "yes" or "no", but more often, especially as there's no pressure to do so, you'll find that people tend to expand a little on the yes or no.

Have you come far?
No, we only live about half a mile away. Almost neighbours!

Compare "Have you come far?" with "Where do you come from?", which sounds more direct and therefore more demanding – though it all depends how you ask it.

> You might fear that asking questions is intrusive. This can also be a generational issue – older people are less inclined to "pry". Think of your simple question as a gift to the other person, an invitation to talk – *if* they want to.

TRY A COMMENT FOLLOWED BY A QUESTION

Putting these two methods together, a comment followed by a question works really well. The comment is just put out there without obligation, and if it is picked up, you can follow with a simple question. For example:

Coldest January on record, they say . . .
Mm yes, freezing . . .

You follow with another comment and a question tagged on the end:

All this snow! We couldn't get out at all last week, could you?

If you feel daunted by initiating a conversation, set yourself the challenge of making a comment or asking a question of someone you don't know. Find an easy context – a shop, restaurant or pub, a queue, a meeting or an event – and make your comment. It has to be a random comment to satisfy the challenge. Just stating your lunch order to a waiter doesn't count!

When you've done it, give yourself a pat on the back whether you got a response or not. The challenge was in the doing, not the result. Of course, if you got a satisfactory response, that's great!

INTRODUCE YOURSELF POSITIVELY

At a social or work event, a good way to break into a conversation can be to take a more formal approach. Smile at someone, extend your hand in greeting and introduce yourself clearly: "Hi, I'm John Smith – pleased to meet you!" Then immediately follow up with a comment or question as before. Your general demeanour will make all the difference – if you look and sound friendly the other person is more likely to respond in a friendly manner.

When you first open your mouth, don't worry about thinking of something clever to say. Your initial approach doesn't have to be original. In fact, the art of small talk – the first important tool in the conversationalist's toolbox – is to start with something simple and everyday – and relevant. Great friendships and valuable connections grow from little conversations!

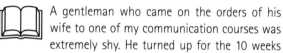 A gentleman who came on the orders of his wife to one of my communication courses was extremely shy. He turned up for the 10 weeks in a row, but scarcely volunteered a word. At the beginning of each session I asked participants for stories of their experiences in communication during the previous week. At the final session the shy gentleman spoke up for the very first time.

> "I spoke to my next-door neighbour over the fence," he offered, diffidently.
> *"What did you say to him,"* I asked.
> "I said hello," he replied.

The group registered this information in amused silence – it seemed minor progress, to say the least. But then I asked him:

> *Have you been neighbours for long?*
> "25 years," he replied. "It's the first time we've ever spoken to each other."

Witnessing his satisfaction, I realized the momentous significance of that first step.

4.2   Keeping the conversation going

Keeping a conversation going is simple. Yet in practice, if you listen to people talking to each other, you'll find it often doesn't happen.

A conversation is like a game of tennis, where questions are the service, and answers the return of ball. Thus, with questions and responses and questions again, the ball is hit to and fro and the conversation flourishes. Good questions keep a conversation moving forward positively.

If you follow your answer with your next question, you keep the ball in play. For example:

> Have you been here before?
> *No, I haven't.* **Have you?**

The answer, "No, I haven't" on its own would close down that particular exchange. "Have you?" sends the ball back to the other person.

Even "No, I haven't" is better than a bald "No" on its own.

 Monosyllables are like nails in the coffin of a conversation.

☞ If monosyllabic answers are your habit, practise responding to questions with more than *yes, no* or *dunno!* Try some of these:

- Yes, I have. Yes, I do. Yes, it is, etc.
- Yes, sometimes. No, not often. Yes, usually. Yes, but not for a long time, etc.
- Yes, we've been coming here for ages. No, I've never seen it before, etc.

Such practice is like oiling the wheels of your voice. You'll find it really helps to get you into a conversation.

ADDING A LITTLE EXTRA

In more elegant play you don't bat the ball right back to the same place it came from, but vary the pace by adding a bit extra each time after the answer.

Have you been here before?
No, I haven't. Do you know this area well?
No, I've never been to Manchester before. Actually, I haven't even been up north much! We live in Devon. And you?
Oh, I come from the south too. I live right on the coast in Dorset. I love the sea. Do you live near the coast too?

And so a conversation slowly grows from safe and unassuming beginnings into something more interesting, and by the time it is going well, no one is really thinking any more in terms of comment, question or answer – it's just flowing.

TAKING IT GENTLY

The art of questioning is to move gently, transitioning smoothly from one thing to another. A question doesn't work well with someone you don't know if it is too sudden, intimate, specific or challenging. Here are a couple of examples of what *not* to do at the outset of a conversation:

> We love living in Devon.
> *So what did you pay for your property there then?*
> (too personal and specific)

> We love living in Devon.
> *Great county – for geriatrics! It's where people go to die really, isn't it?*
> (too challenging to catch the intended humour)

Wait until you have a measure of the other person and have built up some trust before you introduce subjects that attract strong views – like sex, religion, politics and money – unless you like to live dangerously! It's best to build up to controversial subjects rather than launching straight in if you want the other person to feel at ease.

Be a bit careful of humour too. Mostly humour helps a conversation, but if you have a dry sense of humour or humour with an edge to it, it might take the other person a little while to tune in and cause awkward misunderstandings at the outset. Warm up to humour; get a feel of what the other person is like first.

OPEN QUESTIONS

After the initial exchange you'll get more from the other person if you ask questions that invite an explanation rather than a yes or no answer. For example, "How do you find living in Sydney?" rather than "Do you like living in Sydney?" Notice how questions that start with *what* and *how* invite fuller answers:

How do you find working in the city?
What are the challenges of working outdoors?

Questions are essential for conversations, but they're only half the story. A good conversation never feels like a question and answer session; it's less structured than that. Conversational partners take a turn in leading, and good listening keeps the conversation flowing. We look at listening a bit later.

CHANGING THE SUBJECT

It's a great feeling when a conversation starts to flow and gains its own momentum. Often when that happens, you will both happily move from theme to theme without even noticing how that is happening.

At times though, you may find that you want to move on from the current subject, or you might suddenly want to say or ask something that is unconnected. In that case, it's a good idea to pave the way for your new theme so that a sudden change of direction doesn't jolt your partner or confuse them with its "foreign" content. You can do this by adding an introductory sentence. For example:

Do you know, there's something I really want to ask you . . .
Completely changing the subject, I'd like to tell you something
    . . .
Just out of the blue, I was suddenly wondering if . . .
Oh, before I forget, I wanted to tell you . . .

By adding such a sentence the other person – though momentarily surprised by your shift to something new – has time to gather themselves by the time you actually say the core of what you are intending to say.

4.3 Stories

Often a question or comment offers the opportunity for a story. Maybe someone asks about the excitements of sailing. The other person replies,

> It's certainly challenging at times! Last week it was so rough we didn't get more than 100 metres outside the harbour. You can't believe how scary it was! We had to . . .

They are off into an anecdote about sailing. Stories are one of the joys of conversation, and they can be as short as one sentence or as long as a whole narrative. Of course, you can prepare beforehand various stories that others might find interesting, but nothing works as well as stories from your own experience that spring to mind in the context of the conversation. Personal and spontaneous, they add interest to an exchange.

If you feel daunted by conversation, one of the greatest steps forward you can make is to dare to tell a personal anecdote. Don't imagine that your story needs to be entertaining – so long as it's not too long! If it's personal and real that's all you need. A story can inspire other people to think of similar experiences of their own and move the conversation forward positively.

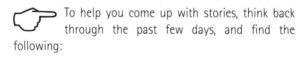 To help you come up with stories, think back through the past few days, and find the following:

- Something that made you smile.
- Something you read or heard on radio or television that you found interesting.

- Something memorable that you heard someone say.
- Something you found surprising.

Now practise telling the story of each out loud. I asked a friend for an example, and he told me this:

> *"I saw something that really made me smile this morning on the way to work. There was a homeless man outside the station, and he'd collected five large cardboard boxes and written a huge letter on each, so that they spelled S M I L E. And people did! There was a really cheerful atmosphere, quite unusual at 8 on a Monday morning!"*

This is a good time to remember that conversation is a game of interaction. If the other person tells a story, it might suddenly remind you of something you'd like to tell them. In fact, you may instantly want to top the other person's story with your own more dramatic and exciting tale. Going back to the sailing story at the start of this section, having heard about the rough sea, one listener interposes:

> *"The sea was rough outside the harbour, was it? You'll never guess what happened to me the last time I went out in my sailing dinghy. It was the most dangerous situation I've ever been in – they even had to scramble a helicopter . . ."*

If you constantly top each other's input, a conversation can easily become a series of isolated and competitive stories, with minimal connection between them. It's better to stick for a while with the other person's story and build on it by asking questions about their experience, rather than overturn it immediately to interrupt with your own story.

When people just use the subject matter as a trigger for their own input without any interest in each other's contributions, that's not conversation. Mind you, it's a familiar ritual in many households after a long day – as Andy Cohen describes:

"Dinner 'conversation' at the Cohens' meant my sister, mom, and I relaying in brutal detail the day's events in a state of amplified hysteria, while my father listened to his own smooth jazz station in his head."

DROPPING CONVERSATIONAL CLUES – AND PICKING THEM UP

People who are skilled at casual conversation often drop the odd comment into an exchange to offer the other person a gentle lead if they wish to take it, like a free gift:

I think I met you at the conference in Singapore didn't I? I seem to remember it was straight after my year in New Zealand and I was on my way back to Europe.

The obvious response would be to answer the direct question:

Yes, it was definitely in Singapore. Interesting conference wasn't it?

But that whole year in New Zealand tossed casually into the sentence sounds interesting, so you might prefer to follow that up instead:

A whole year in New Zealand? What were you doing out there?

And a fascinating exchange might follow.

Sometimes a clue placed in a conversation can build a more intimate connection if you're prepared to pick it up. For example:

A: Oh yes, I like films too. I used to go to the cinema all the time once I found myself on my own. I saw some terrific films . . .

B: (Picking up the clue) *You found yourself on your own?*

A: Yes, I was married for 12 years, but it all came to a rather sticky end, and once on my own I began to really enjoy my own company for the first time . . . it was a good time actually . . .

And suddenly you're on a different level of conversation from chatting about films you've seen.

Picking up clues takes curiosity and awareness. They often appear half-hidden in the waft and weave of something else, and it won't always feel appropriate to follow up on them. It doesn't interrupt the flow of conversation if you fail to pick them up, but if you do, you have the opportunity to develop the conversation into something different and potentially more interesting.

Picking up such personal clues is a risk. But, on the whole, someone drops the mention of something personal into a discussion only when they are prepared to talk about it; and if you go gently it may lead you to an interesting discussion and the chance to get to know the other person better.

As a speaker, dropping clues requires you to dare to reveal genuine information about yourself. Go for it. There are few moves more effective in building trust and connection than revealing truths about yourself.

5

LISTENING

"Courage is what it takes to stand up and speak; courage is also what it takes to sit down and listen."
– Winston Churchill

Most people worry more about what to say in conversation than about how well they listen. Yet much more than half the success of conversation is in listening. Eavesdropping on random conversations you might not think so, as you often hear just a sequence of anecdotes with little evidence of listening. But listening well is what moves a conversation forward organically and makes it satisfying for both those involved.

Writings from the past give the impression that we've never been very good at listening. "We have two ears and one tongue so that we would listen more and talk less", admonished the Greek philosopher Diogenes. "The art of conversation is the art of hearing as well as of being heard", essay writer William Hazlitt reminded his readers in the eighteenth century. There's even a cautionary traditional nursery rhyme:

A wise old owl lived in an oak,
The more he saw the less he spoke,
The less he spoke the more he heard.
Why can't we all be like that wise old bird?

Listening is often mentioned in the context of professional conversations, such as coaching, mentoring, supervising and counselling, but not so much in ordinary conversation where the emphasis – at least in the West – is more on being interesting to listen to and having stories up your sleeve to illustrate your points than on being a good listener.

It is a wonderful gift to be listened to. It's even a new experience for some people. You may assume that you do listen, but good listening is a much rarer quality than we might like to think. In essence it's so simple. All you have to do is listen. But to listen without interference: without drifting, judging, comparing, criticizing, labelling, planning, interpreting . . . ah, that's maybe not so easy!

5.1 How well do you listen?

Try this questionnaire to reflect on your listening skills. Give yourself 5 points for "a lot"; 1 point for "a little", 0 points for not at all, and 3 points for "somewhere in the middle".

When you are in conversation with someone:

1. How well do you keep your focus on what the person is saying?
2. To what extent do you pick up the meaning from the person's tone of voice, emphasis, rhythm and silences?
3. How much do you pick up from the speaker through looking and noticing body language?
4. How much do you pick up what the speaker is feeling?
5. To what extent do you step into the speaker's shoes and imagine what things are like from his point of view?
6. How well do you suspend judgement while you listen?
7. To what extent do you wait for the speaker to finish before interrupting?
8. To what extent do you give indications that you are listening?

How did you rate yourself? A full score is 40! If you score yourself above 20 you're doing pretty well. If your score is 10 or less, you have work to do – or you're a hard scorer!

5.2 What can happen instead of listening

We do many other things instead of listening well. Here are a few. Don't feel bad if you recognize yourself in them, I think all of us can. You'll certainly recognize people you know! Understanding the various activities you indulge in instead of listening gives you a better sense of what listening actually is, and points the way to becoming a better listener yourself.

REHEARSING YOUR OWN PIECE

Perhaps the most common trait in conversation is to half-listen while you work out what you want to say yourself as soon as your chance comes. You can recognize when others are doing this as they tend to increase their non-verbal agreement noises (even as they listen less!) when they want to speak themselves, as if their "mm mm" or "uh huh", increasing in urgency, will stop the flow enough for them to take over.

We have plenty of reasons for wanting to speak rather than listen. Sometimes we have an overwhelming desire to off-load our emotional baggage; or we're keen to impress and want to be the centre of attention. Often we just think that our choice of theme is much the most interesting, or we enjoy talking about ourselves most. Some people say that the primary impulse to have a conversation at all is the desire to talk, the other person's spiel existing only to introduce your own lines. But without listening there is no conversation, just people talking in turn.

How often does someone ask you a question because they want to say something themselves? Very often I suspect! The conversation goes something like this:

How are you?

Fine thanks, and you?

Oh, thanks for asking! Well as a matter of fact, (big breath!) I've been off work for two weeks . . . terrible cold . . . worst ever . . . suspected pneumonia . . . coughing all night . . . zero sleep . . . (show me sympathy, I want some TLC)!

A comment so easily triggers a thought of your own. The other person complains about changes brought in by senior management, and you are suddenly dying to tell them of the awful treatment your own boss is doling out to staff. So, while the other person talks, you run over in your mind all the different ways in which your boss is out of order, so that you can recount them when your turn comes.

When your turn comes? Many people won't even wait for a turn. They'll burst in with:

Oh, you're so right, it's exactly what happened to me too. I . . .

as they seize the baton to tell their own story. Then you might find yourself interrupting back to take the initiative again,

Oh, isn't that always the way? I did just the same thing when . . .

Note how the interruption can often sound like an affirmation of what the first speaker is saying. It's not though, it's a takeover; it's a coup.

> Whenever you listen to someone, notice how often you're thinking about what to talk about when it's your turn. Listening mantra number one is, listening is not "waiting to talk". Listening is listening!

DAYDREAMING

It's easy to lose focus when others are speaking if their manner and tone of voice are dull. Even when the other person speaks in an engaging way about something that interests you, you may find that their words trigger a thought process of your own, and you go off into a reverie.

For example, a friend tells you:

> I've decided to go for the job. My boss thinks I'm ready, and you know, I'm nearly 40, so it's probably about time I . . .

And, interested as you are in your friend's story, you think:

> I'm over 40 myself and I've been in the same job for 15 years. Far too long! I need to summon the courage to go for something else. If only my boss showed an interest. I've always been too timid, and it's held me back . . .

The other person might or might not notice the absent expression that appears in your face . . . you may be there in body, but mind and spirit are elsewhere!

When you find yourself drifting off into your own experience, just notice what is happening and come back gently to listening again. If your internal thought was useful and relevant, remind yourself to pick it up later. You will drift, so don't give yourself a hard time about it; just note and accept it, and come back to listening.

Putting the boot on the other foot, it's useful when you're speaking yourself to remember that people process what you say by referring internally to their own experience. Realizing this, you can allow for it.

PRETENDING TO LISTEN

Some people pretend to listen because they want to speak and be listened to when their turn comes, but don't want to offend you when you are talking by revealing that they are not listening. Parents, overwhelmed by the ability of a small child to talk for England, often become accomplished at pretending to listen. It's amazing how skilled you can get at putting on an appropriate expression and making sympathetic encouraging noises as you lend half an ear to the tone of the child's voice, without attending to what they are actually saying.

People pretend to listen when they've lost the plot. "I nod and smile at him", says Jodi Picoult in *House Rules*. "You'd be surprised at how far that response can get you in a conversation where you are completely confused."

 If you pretend to listen, you might assume that other people don't notice. But they probably do. They are certainly aware subconsciously that something is missing.

NON-LISTENING

Have you experienced someone just not listening at all, and making responses that don't fit? I suspect that it's probably quite common! I remember one conversation with a good friend (who wasn't physically deaf, by the way!) as I pottered around the kitchen:

D'you want a cup of tea?
Mmm, oh yes, nice day.
I thought I might sort through the schedule.

Yes, I go there all the time.
Would you like a million pounds for your birthday? (just testing!)
Yes, ha, ha! You think I'm not listening don't you? Well I am!
Really?

 Check whether people are listening by looking at them now and then. Or shock them into listening, as above!

FILTERING THE COMMUNICATION

It's impossible *not* to filter what we hear. We all hear only a part of what is said, depending on what we notice and how our view of the world colours what we take in. The skill of listening lies in hearing as much as we can without putting our own interpretation on it. If you ignore what you don't want to hear or just listen for what may affect you, you are possibly missing the most important elements of a communication.

For example, your sister or brother tells you that they have suddenly been given the chance of an exciting holiday, and it means that they are not going to be able to visit your elderly mother for a month and the responsibility will fall to you. If you hear *only* the negative impact on yourself, you fail to respond to the fact that your sibling has the chance of an exciting holiday, and he or she won't feel properly heard.

 Two people never hear the same thing. Begin to be aware of just how much you listen according to your interest, assumptions, values and beliefs.

JUDGEMENT

We filter particularly through judgement. It's natural to assess what someone else is saying but this definitely gets in the way of listening. Perhaps the speaker tells you about a bad experience with a plumber they contacted through Yellow Pages, and you think to yourself that you would never have found yourself in that position as you wouldn't have contacted a plumber without personal research and recommendation. So, as you continue to listen, you filter the communication with your judgement and your opinions of yourself and the other person. If you do this, you may well miss the main point of the communication.

Judgement often occurs when a conversation doesn't feel equal. If one person makes it clear that they have a superior role, an essential element of conversation is lost. It doesn't matter whether I am your boss, your elder, more educated or more privileged than you, true listening takes place in the context of equality.

Sometimes people listen with a negative filter permanently switched on. Whatever the speaker says, they think of all the things the speaker *should* have said instead of what they did say, all the things they *ought to* have done instead of what they actually did, and all the things they *should* be thinking and feeling instead of what they *are* thinking and feeling. Inner judgement very quickly turns into unhelpful advice, in language full of those same *shoulds* and *oughts.*

Listen out for the expressions of necessity when you respond to someone, or when they respond to you. For example:

- *You* must *get it fixed.*
- *You* ought to *have told them.*
- *You* should have *stopped it then.*
- *You'll* have to *nip it in the bud.*

Listen out too for *why* expressed sharply. That also suggests judgement.

- *Why did you decide to do that?*
- *Why did you?*
- *Why didn't you?*

 Judgement is often expressed with a label. Beware if you find yourself saying, "You're hopeless!" or "You're too sensitive." It means instant judgement has leapt into play and you're not truly listening any more.

This is often a key problem with families that say they don't talk to each other. When you sense inner criticism the moment you open your mouth, you soon stop sharing thoughts and feelings altogether.

Judgement, whether openly expressed or not, severely inhibits free conversation. Get curious instead.

PLAYING THE PSYCHIATRIST

Another way people fail to listen properly is when they play mind games, and think they know what is going on better than the speaker. Listen out for phrases such as:

- I know exactly what you're talking about.
- I know you. You always undersell yourself.
- Your problem is, you're too timid.

Such phrases tend to introduce those familiar statements of advice – "you should" and "you ought", and "what I would have done"; or moralistic universal statements such as, "That's the wrong approach . . ." and, "The best thing to do is . . .". You're right back in judgement.

> You can never really know what is going on for someone else. The longer you can suspend certainty and closure, the closer you will get to the truth.

REASSURING OR DIVERTING

When a speaker is talking about problems, it sometimes makes for painful listening, and you may be tempted to interrupt to make things better – either by trying to suggest that everything will be okay or by diverting the person to take their mind off things. Such attempts to stop the person from feeling negative emotions can be well meant but in the process negate their experience and stop the flow.

> The question is, whose discomfort are you trying to assuage, the other person's or your own?
>
> Just listening is probably all that's needed in such situations. It's often the biggest gift you can give another human being.

5.3　How to listen well

Clearly, there are many ways we fail to listen to each other in conversation! So how *do* you become a better listener? There are many factors involved. The better you understand other people and yourself, the fewer filters you apply and the better you listen. The greatest listening is to hear all and expect nothing.

Of course you use your ears to listen, and you hear the other person's words. In fact the actual words represent only a small part of the meaning. The person's meaning and intention show up in their tone of voice, pitch, variation in tone, volume, emphasis, rhythm, fullness or lack of breath, pauses, hesitations, what is *not* said and much else besides. Nuanced listening gives you a huge amount of information.

If you can see the person, you can use your eyes to help you understand what you're hearing as you take in movement, gesture, posture, balance, eye movements, skin colour, tensing and relaxing, rigidity and softness.

Body language and voice tone give you greater truth than the actual words spoken, and sometimes even negate the meaning of the actual words. To give an obvious example, imagine for instance the words "Well, that was great!" spoken with slumped shoulders a twisted smile and a flat ironic tone.

Some listeners interpret every statement as if it is logical and focus on facts even when the speaker is grappling with feelings. Doing this they often miss the point, and irritate the speaker with their comments. Listening includes picking up the speaker's underlying emotions, which are an important part of the meaning. It helps to think of listening from the heart rather than only with the head.

We assume that communication is straightforward, but language is in many ways a crude attempt to convey what a speaker intends, and a listener can do with a sixth and seventh sense to interpret what is really going on!

SHOW THAT YOU'RE LISTENING

If someone comes to you in distress and you give no visual or auditory clue that you are listening, don't be surprised if they burst into tears and rush from the room! People thrive on being listened to – but they need to *know* that you're listening. You may be listening really well as you move around the room tidying up your files, but if the speaker doesn't know that you're listening, they lose the invaluable connection that comes from attention. So, give positive visual and auditory clues that you're listening. You will probably do this naturally, but check it out.

 Consider the different ways you can allow the other person to feel heard:

- *If* you are both sitting down, choose a comfortable way to be in relation to each other – for example have the chairs at 45° and not too far apart.
- Settle into yourself. If you feel comfortable, the other person will too. Sit in a way that makes the speaker feel that you are open to listening – not all bunched up with legs crossed and shoulders hunched over folded arms, unless that is how they are sitting.
- Look frequently at the person if they are looking at you as they speak. (If they are looking up or

away to describe something, then join them in their focus.)

- Nod your head or smile in agreement sometimes. As a speaker it's great to feel your listener's appreciation and encouragement.
- Make odd comments or non-verbal sounds to show that you are listening, for example, Really, Oh, Did you? Was it?
- Ask a question when appropriate to help the speaker to continue, for example: What was that like? What happened next?
- Actively receive their message, by asking questions to clarify what you're unsure about, reflecting back to them what you are hearing and encouraging further explanation.

All that is *really* required for listening is your empathetic attention. Your undivided focus on the other person makes them feel accepted and acknowledged – important gifts for them.

5.4 Freeing yourself to listen

You have probably experienced times when you are anxious or stressed and find it impossible to focus properly on what someone is telling you. Listening well depends to a large extent on your state of mind. It's different for different people. What allows *you* to listen well?

 Ask yourself these simple questions:

- What enables you to listen well?
- What gets in the way of good listening?
- How are you when you're really listening?

Take your time to think about it. Remember how you are in yourself when you're *really* listening to someone. Consider what blocks you or distracts you from listening well. How are you when you are 100% intent on what the other person is trying to communicate? Jot down your answers if you like, and answer for yourself before reading further.

Here's what one respondent said:

What enables you to listen well?

I think it's a feeling of being open without prejudice. I listen when I'm curious, and that happens when I'm interested in the person. Actually, I mostly am interested in people – just things get in the way sometimes.

I listen when I'm relaxed and at ease with myself. So I find that if I consciously let go of tension and breathe I listen better. I also find it important to focus just on hearing the person – where they're coming from and what their intention is – and not on how I'm going to respond, because when I listen well I'm confident I'll know what to say next without having to think about it. I also find it helps to be aware that listening is a whole body activity, not just brain stuff, so I settle into myself and even imagine that it's my heart and gut listening, rather than my intellectual brain.

What gets in the way of good listening?

Oh, lots of things! Sometimes I'm not in a good state of mind and don't really have time for it. Sometimes I get a bit judgemental about what's being said; sometimes I get distracted. If I'm trying too hard to do a good job of listening I get a sort of performance anxiety and don't listen very well.

How are you when you are really listening?

(After a pause) You know, I think it's being at peace – knowing that I'm okay. So there's nothing I have to do – like sympathizing, coming up with ideas or anything else. I can just be, knowing that I'm in the right place and it's going to be all right, and I'll have all the answers I need at the right time . . . does that make sense?

I wonder what your responses will be when you answer for yourself. They'll be personal to you. Take your time, and just see what comes up for you.

To listen really well is a skill, and like all skills it develops with practice. The fourteenth-century Persian poet Hafiz wrote a little poem about listening:

> *How*
> *Do I*
> *Listen to others?*
> *As if everyone were my Master*
> *Speaking to me*
> *His*
> *Cherished*
> *Last*
> *Words.*

5.5 Deep listening

We know from neuroscience that when we listen we respond not just with thinking in the brain but with stomach, heart and gut. When you listen to someone not only with your ears and eyes but also open your heart and gut to them, you begin to hear more of what is going on, beyond the actual words. You capture the deeper story – the message beneath the message.

You discover that what is actually said is only the surface structure of any communication. The deeper truth lies beneath. For example, someone says, "Yes, I want to", and with deep listening you hear the underlying feelings too, "Yes, I want to but I'm afraid", or "Yes, I want to but I feel guilty". You sense anger beneath a righteous statement, hopelessness beneath a tirade or vulnerability beneath assertiveness. You also increase your sensibility to atmosphere. You are better able to read an occasion, and respond intuitively to the truth of what is going on rather than what is presented on the surface.

To do this it helps to maintain a soft focus, absorbing the big picture rather than focusing on details or precise interpretations of the actual words. With a soft focus, you pick up messages beneath the surface. For instance, you may hear angry words as the person complains about being let down. But if you temporarily postpone the desire to make sense of the words, and instead just keep breathing and staying open, you sense a different emotion beneath the anger – sadness or fear for instance. There is frequently a presenting story and another story *behind* the story.

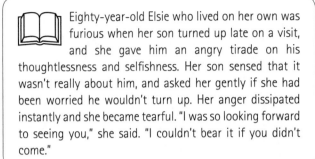

Eighty-year-old Elsie who lived on her own was furious when her son turned up late on a visit, and she gave him an angry tirade on his thoughtlessness and selfishness. Her son sensed that it wasn't really about him, and asked her gently if she had been worried he wouldn't turn up. Her anger dissipated instantly and she became tearful. "I was so looking forward to seeing you," she said. "I couldn't bear it if you didn't come."

Be aware of factors that get in the way of deep listening.

- Wanting to make sense too quickly of what's being said.
- Wanting answers, and feeling uncomfortable with not knowing.
- A desire to lead the situation.

Deep listening is possible when you are fully present in mind and body and at ease. As you breathe without tension, your conscious and subconscious absorb multiple layers of information and you understand more than you hear. When that happens you have a strong feeling of connection and the sensation of being in flow – a great experience.

Part Two

The Power of Conversation

6

INFLUENCING A CONVERSATION

"Affect others profoundly: the more you touch others, the better."
– Thomas Leonard

Much of the time, when people chat to each other they're not thinking about a specific outcome – conversation just seems to happen! But people who are skilled in conversation are far from random when they chat. They hold an intention or intentions, usually unspoken, which influence the course their conversation takes. This can be a specific outcome they have in mind, or it may be something as intangible as a guiding quality or attitude.

When Oprah called some people "radiators", she was in fact describing people who have this special skill of affecting a conversation. They might not give it a name, but in what they say and how they listen they demonstrate intentionality. One person I would call a radiator once told me, "I just want to leave the other person better than I find them." Another said, "I always want to be able give the other person something, whether it's interesting information, an enjoyable time, or some sort of help." This kind of intentionality doesn't have to be planned in advance – it's more an attitude of mind that guides you.

> In conversation, you are always sailing into the spontaneous unknown – that's the fun of it – and at the same time, with your intention, you can set your sail in a particular direction.

Whether you are working towards a specific outcome or not, invisible factors – such as your attitude – make all the difference when you want to influence a conversation. The way you view and remember other people profoundly affects any communication with them. If you think that people are basically honest and well meaning, you get one experience. If you think they are not to be trusted and are out to exploit you, you get a different one. Similarly, if you view the world as a place where there's enough to go round and plenty of good things are free, that attitude will create one outcome; and if you believe there's not enough to go around and that everything has to be fought over in fierce competition, then you'll get a different one.

6.1   Know your intention

SPECIFIC OUTCOMES

Often you have a specific outcome in mind when holding a conversation, for example:

- Obtaining information.
- Exchanging opinions and learning new facts.
- Obtaining agreement through negotiation.
- Selling a product or persuading of an idea.
- Influencing the other person's state of mind, through motivating, inspiring, reassuring, galvanizing and so on.

Often the purpose is about connection:

- Making a new friend.
- Improving a relationship.
- Becoming more intimate.
- Accepting, supporting and caring.

Enjoyment may be a guide:

- Creating enjoyment for both of you.
- Having a good laugh.
- Sharing good things.

A conversation goes well when the two parties share a common purpose, even when it's simple and unstated – to have fun or relax together, for instance. The purpose can change as you progress, but the conversation will flow best if you're travelling in a similar direction.

> **!** If one person imagines the conversation is about having a laugh, and the other wants to share some intense feelings, they'll both need to make some adjustment to achieve a satisfying conversation!

 In a reality television programme about the UK's National Health Service, two young men, joking and teasing each other, came into hospital to visit their friend who had had a serious accident. Hearing that the injured man had damaged one of his testicles so badly that he might lose it, the two young men attempted jokes with him about his private parts, but their banter failed to provoke the usual humorous rebuttals, and the conversation dwindled into an awkward silence. Without their usual habit of banter and teasing, they were unable to find a point of connection. They needed a new language of compassion, but it was unknown territory and they failed to find it on that occasion.

VALUES AS INTENTION

Your values can work like hidden intentions to guide you. When you know what is important to you, you can sense when a conversation has trodden on your values, and take steps to steer it back on track. For example, if a guiding value for you is positivity, and the other person has been complaining for a while, you'll want to steer the conversation towards more positive subjects. Or if you have a strong value about trust, and the other person is being economical with the truth, you'll find ways to challenge this.

Think about actual conversations you have with different people, and take your time to reflect on your outcomes for each – including values or principles.

Tony reflected in this way on his meetings with a good friend he saw for a drink every few weeks. They always had plenty to talk about and he realized that the meetings were about enjoyment, and support too, for they were very open with each other about what was going on in their lives. He realized that intellectual stimulation was one of his outcomes and he enjoyed their conversation most when they were exchanging ideas.

Felix had a strong value about openness and trust. His manager was explaining a cost-saving change in the payment system that was going to create late payments for staff. The change would particularly affect employees who had low pay and little job security. The manager suggested disingenuously that employees would gain through more efficient online systems. Feeling somewhat intimidated by his manager's confident words, Felix was still determined to keep the conversation moving truthfully. So, with considerable trepidation but strong intention, he expressed his concern about the impact on workers and suggested interim payments to soften the impact. His manager blustered angrily that change happens and you can't cover for every eventuality. But the strong intention of Felix's words hit home, and eventually the low-paid employees were helped during the transition.

Knowing your overall outcome allows you to be appropriate in a conversation, and guides you towards a fruitful exchange. It also acts as a barometer to flag up when a conversation has lost its way.

6.2 Leading through connection

So, what do you do or say to influence a conversation and steer it towards your desired outcome?

Connection is the magic ingredient of influence. If you connect well with people it takes the smallest lead to influence their state of mind. It's like walking side by side with a good friend. You naturally find yourselves falling into step, and when that happens the smallest intention on your part influences the direction you take together. Usually the other person doesn't even notice a decision has been made as you turn together towards the left or the right.

Once you feel comfortably in tune with each other in conversation, you influence the other person chiefly by the energy of your state of mind. So, if you want the other person to feel motivated, you become enthusiastic yourself, and that quality is transmitted to your partner. If you want him to feel peaceful, you find that calm within yourself.

Sixty-year-old Jenny told me about the day long ago when her father had told her the "facts of life". He wanted to convey to her that love and sex were good, pleasurable and natural, but was himself so stiff, formal and intensely embarrassed as he attempted to communicate, that she can remember to this day the acute discomfort of the situation. She picked up on the tension and embarrassment and he achieved the opposite result from the one intended! She contrasted this experience with later fun conversations behind the bike sheds at school where one girl would giggle urgently, "You'll never guess!" and the others would all crowd around enthusiastically to hear the latest "fact of life". It was there that she learned what her father had wanted to convey rather than in his stilted conversation.

It helps to be clear with yourself about your intention. That's not always as straightforward as it might seem and it's worth spending time to uncover any hidden intentions. If you have words with a colleague in an attempt to heal a rift between you, do you *actually* want peace and harmony, or deep down do you want your colleague to feel as bad as you've been feeling? Life has a funny way of giving you your hidden desires and then somehow surprising you in the process!

 It's useful to pause for a moment before certain conversations and ask yourself, "What do I *really* want from this conversation?"

Sometimes, people fake connection in order to achieve a particular outcome – a sale for instance, or to gain information. But if you use the arts of connection merely to manipulate a result, people tend to be aware of it at some level and feel exploited. They might not show their awareness at the time as the full impact often hits later, but your underlying intentions are not as hidden as you think.

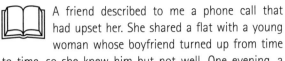 A friend described to me a phone call that had upset her. She shared a flat with a young woman whose boyfriend turned up from time to time, so she knew him but not well. One evening, a year after she had moved away and lost touch with her flatmate, the boyfriend called her, and spent at least 15 minutes asking her with great friendliness how she was and what she was doing. She responded openly and warmly. Then he suddenly interrupted her and interjected, "Oh, by the way, as I'm on the phone . . ." and proceeded to ask her a large favour that would help him in his business. The moment he had the information he was looking for, he ended the conversation brusquely. My friend said the penny dropped for her like a stone as she realized that the chatter had just been a "softening up" to get the introduction he was looking for. "I lost trust through that experience", she confessed.

Connection builds from genuine interest and acknowledgement of the other person: the more truthful the connection, the stronger the potential influence.

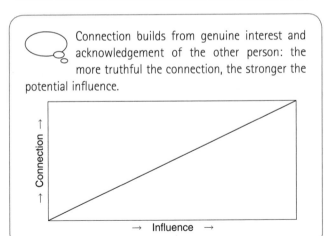

6.3   Creating positive movement

One very effective way to get the best out of conversations is to have your positive sensor engaged. The idea behind the positive sensor is that focusing on what you want gives you more of what you want. When you focus on what's wrong, what has to be fixed and what needs solving, your attention on deficiency puts the spotlight on negatives, and takes you to past problems and difficulties, thus increasing your chance of failure. When instead you focus on the positive, you look for solutions and make much more rapid progress towards what you want.

When you listen with your positive sensor engaged, you become aware that some people use negative language all the time! You ask them about their friends and they tell you about the ways people have betrayed them; you ask them about holidays and they tell you of a friend who's unable to go on holiday because of a nasty accident. Instead of getting mired in their problems, set your compass towards the future and positive change, and think how you'll move the person towards a positive outcome.

☞ Try this out in a conversation with someone. As you listen to the other person, look towards a more positive future, and ask a question that takes the conversation in that direction. When you hear a negative statement, think forward – "Where from here?" rather than backward to a problematic past – "Why did this disaster happen?"

Here are a few examples:

NEG: It's so frustrating that our departments don't communicate with each other.

POS: *If we managed to improve communication, what might be possible then?*

NEG: There's such chaos at home; nobody does anything to help!
POS: *What would you like to happen?*

NEG: I know she's just taking me for a ride.
POS: *How else might you look at this?*

NEG: The bank's in trouble and I'm ruined!
POS: *What can help you in this situation?*

You need to choose your moment for such questions. Sometimes the other person needs a bit of time to tell their story and sense your empathy with their situation before they can accept a question that moves them towards the positive.

 Be careful not to discount the other person's negative statement. Accept that they are expressing their truth, *and* gently influence the conversation towards the positive.

Here are some other general questions that point the conversation in a positive direction:

- What do you want?
- What's the way forward from here?
- How will you do it?
- What's possible now?

The word "if" is particularly effective in leading you towards a better future:

- If it did work out okay, how would that be?
- If you knew the answer, how would you move things forward?
- If you did get the job, what is the first thing you will do?
- If you felt brave enough, how will you proceed?

You might notice that the last two examples have slightly strange grammar. You might say "If you felt brave enough, how *would* you proceed?" But "How *will* you proceed?" suggests positively that you are already brave enough . . . a grammatical sleight of hand.

Each of these questions starts by assuming a successful outcome. Finding questions that move forwards is a skill much used in coaching and cognitive therapy, and you can find many other examples of good questions in coaching literature.

 Your intention is like a magnet drawing you both towards it. By painting a brighter future, you create something attractive that draws you both in.

6.4   Influence can be as gentle as a story

Conversation is one of the greatest agents of change – and the gentlest. Some people see power as hierarchical, but whatever your role you have the potential to create change through conversation. If you keep your eye on your goal, ask good questions and give authentic answers, you often have leverage to change the way other people see things, even if they are more senior or experienced than you are.

As long as you have an intention, you don't need to get agreement on every topic or have the last word. In fact, accepting what other people have to say (not necessarily agreeing) and acknowledging their statements where possible helps the other person to feel connected – as long as you are authentic in what you say. Finding positive ways to help the other person also helps you both move forward to a good outcome.

Stories are effective magnets to inspire, influence and motivate people. A good story draws you in, and moves you subtly towards new possibilities.

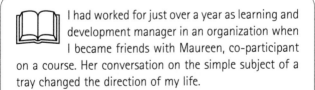 I had worked for just over a year as learning and development manager in an organization when I became friends with Maureen, co-participant on a course. Her conversation on the simple subject of a tray changed the direction of my life.

We were chatting, and Maureen asked me if I had ever seen those beautiful black lacquered Japanese trays with gold engraving. I said I thought I had.

"How much would you pay for one in a car boot sale, if you spotted it amongst all the clutter", she asked me.

"Oh, I don't know, maybe £10", I hazarded.

"What about if you saw one in a large store in the city centre?" she asked.

"Oh, probably £70 or £80", I guessed.

What about if you saw that tray as the only item on display in the window of one of the exclusive antique shops in London's Mayfair?

I imagined the tray beautifully displayed and subtly lit, with the gold shining softly.

"I think it might well be a few thousand pounds", I replied.

"Exactly so," said Maureen. "It's all about the right environment."

I don't think she ever said, "This applies to you too", but the story softly implanted itself in me and I understood that was what she meant. I realized that I wasn't able to fulfil my potential in my current job; and with the picture of that glowing tray in its window often in my mind, within the next three months I'd resigned from my job, and started my own business – never to look back.

☞ Look out for stories you like and collect them to use when appropriate. Remember things that have happened to you, and relive them in your mind as if you are back in that time and place, so that you'll be able to tell them as vivid stories later. Practise telling stories to all who will listen. If you know any children who would enjoy a bedtime story, borrow them if you can! Story telling is a skill that blossoms the more you do it. A story can often be influential when direct advice would fail. Its messages are absorbed by the subconscious and work gently and powerfully.

A story can be as short as a single metaphor or simile. A while ago, someone boosted my confidence enormously when she said, "You're like a light in the dark to me. I'd lost my way, but now I can see where I'm going."

Influence works quietly in many different ways. Sometimes a particular look or tone of voice can make all the difference to how a statement "lands" on the listener. Your state of mind exerts a powerful influence. A silence speaks volumes. With influence, subtlety is key.

Influence grows from connection and trust. When you meet people for the first time, the opportunity to build trust and create a connection is best approached step by step. You don't gain trust by leaping into a conversation with a stranger with instant big questions such as, "So who are you – really, deep down?" or "Tell me, how do you intend to change the world?" Rather, you gain trust by starting with topics that do not demand too much self-revelation, and then move gently towards subjects that are more personal and matter more deeply to you and the other person. As you proceed, you can always be ready to go back a step if the other person fails to respond.

These different levels of conversation are the subject of the next chapter.

7

DIFFERENT KINDS OF CONVERSATION

With a subject as large as conversation, there are clearly many different ways you can communicate, according to context, subject matter, purpose and much else. However, it is also true that each of us has a typical range, and that may not vary currently as much as you might like to think.

 Here are three questions for you:

- Which three or four words would best describe a typical conversation within your family?
- Which three or four words would best describe a typical conversation in a work context?
- Which three or four words would best describe a typical conversation with a good friend?

Answer for yourself before you read further.

I asked a couple of people these questions and got the following answers:

FAMILY: Person A – *Hurried, bossy, practical*
Person B – Warm, casual, intimate

WORK: Person A – *To-the-point, impersonal, technical*
         Person B – Helpful, supportive, interested
FRIENDS: Person A – *Humorous, sarcastic, competitive*
         Person B – Gossipy, emotional, draining

It was a useful reminder of how different our experiences can be with different people!

 When you look at your own answers to the previous questions, ask yourself:

- What are the differences in the way I talk to different people?
- What characteristics of my conversation might I transfer from one sector of my life to another to get better results?

For example, perhaps you are supportive with your children at home, but dictatorial at work. Reflect on how you might you use that ability to be supportive in conversation to good effect at work as well as at home. Maybe you are direct and easy to understand at work, yet at home constantly beat around the bush. Imagine speaking more directly at home and how that might change the responses you get.

In this chapter, I describe various different kinds of conversation. Each has its own characteristics and uses. You discover how to expand your range to different kinds of conversation, and how to move subtly from one to another, to enhance your relationships and achieve your outcomes with people.

In exploring different models of conversation, you find out how not to get stuck in one kind of conversation and you discover exciting possibilities of connection and deeper meaning that emerge as you shift from one to another. Discussion of the weather is clearly not exactly pillow talk for most people, but how do you get on to intimate subjects? I describe different models of talk to you, and then show you how to progress from one to another to find the kind of talk that is satisfying for both of you and connects you more closely with each other.

I've divided the chapter into five kinds of talk:

- Thing Talk
- Action Talk
- Head Talk
- Heart Talk
- Soul Talk

In general conversation or networking, the conversation tends to shift naturally from one kind of talk to another in a free and fluid way. If you have an awareness of how the shifts happen, you can purposefully move an exchange forward when it gets stuck, or shift it to a level that is more gratifying to both of you.

7.1 Thing talk

"A hundred new gadgets to play with.
I couldn't be bothered to wait.
The moment I plugged them all in, though,
it blew every fuse in the state."

– Kenn Nesbitt

When you meet people for the first time, what do you say to them? Most of us choose a safe and non-intrusive impersonal comment, such as, "How was your journey?" or "Have you been here before?"

"How was your journey?" might then develop naturally into a discussion of the car you drove to get here, how well it performs and its petrol consumption: a fine conversation if you're both interested in cars.

I call such impersonal conversation "Thing Talk". This kind of conversation can be interesting and informative, and you'll probably slip into it naturally if you try to make connection with someone through finding a topic in common. You talk about something outside you both without the need either to disclose or elicit personal information. It's general purpose and usually pretty safe. It won't tell you much about the other person, but it makes a good starting point for moving to something more personal if you want.

Some conversation gurus recommend using more adventurous and more personal openings to show that you are an upbeat and interesting person. But plunging in with "So what makes you tick?" or "Do you personally believe in capital punishment?" can easily backfire when you don't know who you're talking to. So, beginning with Thing Talk gives you a solid impersonal base to start off from.

What does Thing Talk include?

Things of course: cars, boats, tools, computers, gizmos, household appliances, travel, houses, clothes, garden furniture, embroidery and every sort of *widget, wotsit* and *thingamajig.*

Typical questions might be:

- How does your new Skoda perform?
- I see you've got the latest smartphone. What new features does it have?
- A holiday home in Austria! In what area?

Notice that the form of question as well as the subject matter is impersonal. For example, "How does your car perform?" rather than "Why on earth do you like Skodas?"

Topics of time and place:

- Been here before? (the classic chat-up line!)
- How long does it take you to get to work?
- Where do you get the best bargains?

Information:

- What's the latest on that Scottish murder enquiry?
- I heard the new government bonds are almost sold out already – what do you know about them?
- Have you any idea what the new shop on the green is selling?

Activities, treated impersonally:

- Have you seen the new Bond movie?
- Where's the next game on the rugby tour, do you know?
- Apparently the New Year fireworks are going to be the most expensive ever. Have you heard what theme they've chosen?

Learning and facts:

- Apparently some autonomous cars are to be marketed this year – the price is still high though, isn't it?
- Have you seen the fresh tactics of our new national football or baseball trainer?
- Are you interested in the history of religious art?
- This year is the hottest ever recorded on our planet; do you follow the data on global warming?

Humour of a general nature:

- Have you heard the one about . . . ?
- Did you hear what the Chancellor said yesterday by mistake?!
- Did you see that man with red underpants outside his trousers?!

Talking about external matters can be very pleasurable when you find a topic that interests both of you. When you focus on something external, companionship builds around the shared interest without necessarily allowing you to know each other better. It can be an opportunity for fun and humour. It can also be deadly serious, informative or enlightening.

Numerous friendships stretch back decades, where two people know practically nothing about each other apart from the single fact that they both play golf, collect stamps, have an interest in industrial history or whatever their shared interest offers. That, for many people, is the pleasure of it.

Some of the most exciting scientific discoveries have been the outcome of conversations between experts of different disciplines. The discovery of DNA came about through endless conversations between Crick, a physicist and Watson, a biologist, each coming from a different discipline and viewpoint. Crick used to say that he needed to simplify things for himself through simple questions, and discussions yielded valuable new insights. After the discovery of DNA, Watson said, "Discovery happens not by accident but by the careful assembling of a group of people who . . . know a lot about a lot of different things." He noted that a brilliant fellow scientist, Lars Paulin, engaged with the same problem, was hampered in his ability to figure things out by the fact that he was working on his own. Conversation was important to the scientific break-through.

I'll come back to this idea of important conversations. For now, it's good to know that conversations about things can be exciting in terms of facts, and less useful in terms of connecting on an intimate level with another human being.

7.2 Action talk

"There's nothing . . . absolutely nothing . . . half so much worth doing as simply messing around in boats."
– Kenneth Grahame, *The Wind in the Willows*

Perhaps the second most common question after "Have you been here before?" is "What do you do?" That's "Action Talk". Action questions give you a picture of the person *doing* things, without them having to reveal what is going on inside their head or heart.

The action question is basically "What do you do?" in all its numerous variations and formats:

- What do you do for a living?
- What are your main responsibilities at work?
- How do you spend your free time?
- What do you do on holiday?

Such questions invite personal stories, and many conversations of this kind turn into an exchange of anecdotes. In answer to one of the questions above, the person responds with a story:

"My favourite sport is American football. I play quarterback. My team got to the regional finals this year. It was such a close match – we so nearly won. If it hadn't been for penalty time and a referee with a blind spot . . ."

Maybe the first person also plays football and has an equivalent football anecdote to relate. Or he plays cricket, and comes up with an experience of that game. For the conversation to be interesting to both parties, you need to find connections between your stories. If they have little relation to each other the conversation never really moves on. You're like two spinning cogs that never manage to engage each other.

Such conversations take good listening, for if both of you are keener to entertain with your own story than to hear the other person's, it's not very satisfying. Even with good listening, a whole evening of action stories can pall. The author Neil Postman suggests that it's all stories now: "Americans no longer talk to each other, they entertain each other." He glumly calls his book, *Amusing Ourselves to Death.*

Storytelling can get competitive too. I was at Pilates, waiting for a previous class to finish, and I listened as one old lady told us about how happy she was that a stray cat had adopted her and now lived in her house. Before she'd finished, someone interrupted with her own cat story about a neighbour's cat that got stuck up a tree. The fire brigade was called and played their hose on the cat to encourage it down, but with such vigour that the cat fell, broke its back and had to be put down. Her dire account completely wiped out the first story and disturbed her listeners, so that everyone sidled into the training room with relief when the previous class finished. It isn't enough to have a theme in common. Stories work best when the narrators acknowledge what's gone before and don't try to outdo each other!

THE ART OF SMALL TALK

You can engage very easily with someone you meet for the first time using a combination of Action Talk and Thing Talk. Take this short exchange:

> Where are you going on holiday this year? (Thing Talk)
> *The south coast as usual. We always go to Chichester Harbour – we've got a boat there.* (Thing Talk)
> Oh, what've you got? (Thing Talk)
> *It's a J/92 sailboat; we entered Cowes Week with it this year.* (Thing to Action Talk)
> Oh, how did you do? (Action Talk)
> *We were runner up in our class. Good result! Do you sail?* (Action Talk)

Small talk gives you social bonding whilst still maintaining a certain degree of personal distance. Nothing gets too emotional or intimate – it's conversation with a light touch. Humour belongs here, as long as it's used to lighten the conversation, not to get personal.

Action Talk has an important place at social occasions. When you want to bring other people into a group conversation, you might introduce them with Action Talk.

> Hello everyone, this is Stephanie; she's doing neuro-research at Manchester University, but has just spent the summer cockle picking on the Lancashire coast.

Action Talk can be a good source of information. If you are wondering whether to train to be a political journalist, you'll find it useful to talk to a current journalist and ask them what they did to get the job in the first place and exactly what they do in their role day by day. If you want to walk the Inca Trail and know friends who've already done it, what better than ask them what arrangements they made, what they took with them, and what they did when the weather was bad?

It can also be an important stepping-stone to more personal talk. It may provide a surface structure while other things are going on underneath, such as looks, feelings and intuition.

7.3 Head talk

"*Great minds discuss ideas; average minds discuss events; small minds discuss people.*"
– Eleanor Roosevelt

Action Talk is about what a person does; Head Talk is about their *thinking*. If you start by asking someone what they do, and then move on to how they succeed at what they do, the skills and qualities they use, how they view certain situations and the choices they make, you are moving on to Head Talk. It includes:

Thoughts:

- How's the best way to tackle this issue, do you think?
- What do you think about the decision to go for a new communications system?
- What do you think he meant by that phrase?

Opinions:

- What's your opinion of the new recipe?
- What do you think of using self-reinforced thermoplastics in the building?
- What's the future of politics in our country, in your opinion?

Skills and know-how:

- How is it that you never get lost when you're trekking?
- How did you become such a confident speaker?
- How do you stay calm when the pressure's on?

You move from Action Talk to Head Talk by asking a more personal "how" question about an action, or by eliciting someone's thoughts and opinions on the subject:

> So you play chess in a league? (Action Talk). How did you get to that standard? (Head Talk).

A question of one type doesn't guarantee a reply at the same level. The responder in the last example might stay with action:

> Well, I've played five times a week for a decade and more.

Or the person might follow your lead and respond in Head Talk:

> I think it's about focusing and keeping going. I never let myself get put off by losing – even when I lost all the time!

With the latter response, you get to know more about this chess player as a person. Hearing about his resilience, you might start to wonder about how resilient he is in other parts of his life, or what that ability to focus says about him. You are building a fuller picture of him as a person, and this gives you the chance to understand him better and to develop the conversation in other directions if you choose.

CAPABILITIES

The easiest step from Action Talk to Head Talk is to ask someone *how* they do something.

So you play chess? How do you keep all the possible choices of move in your head?

How do you stay so calm when everything's falling to pieces around you?

EXCHANGE OF IDEAS

In addition to enjoying the interchange of capabilities and skills, you learn more about people's inner worlds through Head Talk. You gain access to their cognitive skills, their mental maps and strategies, their abilities and their personal opinions. Once you have made an initial connection and both feel comfortable to express thoughts and opinions, questions such as those previously listed can open up rich avenues of intellectual conversation.

Intellectual stimulation and debate go back 1500 years to the tradition of critical enquiry described by Plato, which questions, asks for reasons for choices and explores abstract themes.

Before our age of information, intellectual conversation was a major source of learning too. Jane Austen was surely speaking for herself when her heroine Anne Elliot in *Persuasion* declares, "My idea of good company, Mr Elliot, is the company of clever, well-informed people, who have a great deal of conversations."

In our own day, Head Talk is particularly valued in the workplace, and people who excel at it are considered intelligent. Young people who are lucky enough to learn the art of debate at school and have the opportunity to try out their ideas and opinions, have a ready advantage later in the world of work.

EXCHANGE OF OPINIONS

One element of Head Talk is especially alive and well today, and that is the expression of opinions. At meetings and parties, in pubs, coffee shops and in the media, we hear endlessly: "I think this"; "Well I think that"; "Well, no, it's like this"; "I think you'll find it's like that". Such remarks are not always qualified with "I think", "in my opinion" or "in my view" either, but are more often aired as unsubstantiated universal statements.

When you exchange opinions in a personal conversation with someone, you reveal information about yourself, and you get to know the other person as they share their opinions honestly with you. Friendships and strong business alliances grow through shared opinions and lively debate:

Banks are entirely to blame for the economic crisis.
Yes, and the government is trying hard to convince us otherwise.

I hate intensive farming!
I agree – it's ruining the countryside.

I hold that there's more truth in a novel than in a newspaper.
Oh, I don't think so – real life must reveal more truth, mustn't it?

Opinions are a common method of persuasion in sales. Notice the absence of "in our view" here:

This is the best heating system on the market.
This phone would rank highest in any survey you cared to undertake.
It's simply the best sports car in the world, no question.

WIT

Wit is one of the delights of Head Talk. Clever plays on words, jokes, banter and raillery all contribute to the to and fro of conversation, and often signal that people are comfortable enough to mock and tease each other. Without empathy, however, it can easily be misjudged, and often keeps people at a distance from each other. Shakespeare, as usual a good judge of human emotions, has Beatrice and Benedick in *Much Ado About Nothing* indulge in witty banter with each other in order to connect – at a distance. Their romantic relationship only blossoms when the banter stops.

7.4 Heart talk

"People will forget what you said, people will forget what you did, but people will never forget how you made them feel."
– Maya Angelou

Heart Talk is about discovering what matters to people. You ask a question and – if they feel safe and comfortable – they tell you what's important to them, what gives them motivation and energy, and what gives their life meaning. They tell you how they *feel* about it.

Questions in this mode include:

What matters:

- What really matters to you about working with teenagers?
- What's important for you about your job?

Meaning:

- What would this opportunity mean for you?
- What does it mean for you to give up your job to care for your father?

Values:

- Why did you start working in prisons?
- How do you make the children feel valued?

Feelings (it's all about feelings . . .):

- How do you feel when you're skiing in fresh snow up in the high mountains?
- How does it feel when your team's working well together?

When you ask such questions, tune in to what people might be feeling and give them space and time to answer. Conversations of the heart usually grow organically out of everyday conversations when you've built trust. When you ask someone about what they care about *and they know that you care*, they will answer you from the heart.

Karl asked his friend Mary what she had done in the summer, and she replied that she'd been walking in Scotland. He asked, "Why Scotland?" She told him it was somewhere she went all the time. There was something about the way she said it that gave him the feeling she was deeply fond of the country, and so he asked gently, "What is it about Scotland – for you?" She paused. "I'm not sure," she said, "It's . . ." She seemed to struggle for words for a moment. "It's a place where I always feel happy. Whether it's the wide, open spaces, the quiet, the mountains . . . I don't quite know. I just know that I breathe that crisp air and a calm comes over me; I feel I've come home."

The way Karl asked his second question gave Mary the impression that he was genuinely interested in how she *felt*, so she answered him from the heart. If a work colleague, not particularly interested, had asked brightly, "What is it about Scotland?" she would have answered with Thing Talk or Action Talk. "Oh, you know, the scenery is magnificent, and I enjoy walking in the hills." The colleague would then not have learned as much about her as Karl did.

When feelings and values play a major part in a conversation, you reach a stage where conversation becomes especially enjoyable and worthwhile to both of you. Some people talk about a conversation that has a "buzz". It's the kind of conversation that happens most often between intimate friends, but it can also happen with strangers if both of you are open enough to touch on meanings and beliefs and find that you share values.

Asking people what they enjoy is a great way to discover their values, and can be asked at any stage in a conversation.

The next time you meet someone for the first time, if you decide to ask "What do you do for a living?" follow it up with, "What do you enjoy about it?" Note the kind of reply you receive. Try these and similar questions too:

Why do you love building websites?
What do you enjoy about being by the sea?
What's the best thing for you about horse riding?

If you ask with genuine interest and empathy, you'll probably hear an answer that tells you what matters to the person:

Websites? I find problem-solving exciting and satisfying – there's always an answer if you look hard enough!
The sea? I feel free by the ocean. It's always changing, and it gives me a strong sense of the wildness and power of nature.
Horse riding? Horses are the gentlest, most intuitive animals – I appreciate their understanding and empathy.

The enjoyment question is great for speed dating! Ask a Heart Talk question with empathy and you'll not only find out more about the other person, but you'll probably draw closer too.

EMOTIONAL SUPPORT

The language of feeling can be a great emotional support for people. If the other speaker in a conversation uses feeling language, they will sense your support if you use feeling language too. You will completely fail to connect if you leap immediately to practical responses with Thing Talk and Action Talk before you have acknowledged what they are feeling. If, on the other hand, you reply first from the heart, the other person will appreciate your support, and be more ready for practical solutions in good time.

How *not* to do it:

> I'm feeling a bit sad now my daughter's gone.
> Go for a brisk walk; that usually takes one's mind off things.

Someone looking for emotional support is usually capable of finding their own solutions to problems. Their immediate need is to share what they are feeling and sense that you care. The language of logic is more likely to irritate than to prove helpful at a moment when someone is full of feeling.

Incidentally, you can miss each other in the opposite direction too. "Sorry, I missed my train," said Stephen casually to his coach as he arrived late for his appointment. "How do you *feel* about missing that train?" his coach asked in a deeply sympathetic voice. Stephen was instantly irritated and snapped, "Not *everything's* about feelings you know. No one's died – I just missed my train!"

INTIMATE CONVERSATION

If you want to become closer to someone, there will always come a time to leave behind talk of doing and thinking and engage in conversation about things that affect you both more deeply.

Take the simple question a close friend might ask, "How are you?"

You could stay away from feelings by telling the friend what you've been doing:

> I've been working 18-hour days, persuading my mother at last to move into a care home, and at the same time getting the new policy bedded down at work against considerable opposition.

Such a response is likely to lead to more talk about difficulties at work and awkward relatives. But if the question is genuine and heart-felt, a more personal – and truthful – answer would touch on sadness and being overwhelmed, and bring a closer understanding between you.

Pearl couldn't understand why she found it so difficult to find a partner to share her life with. She was outgoing and met people often in her work and leisure activities. Pearl's friends thought they knew why. Firstly, Pearl loved an argument, so whenever she got into conversation with someone for the first time, she pushed her point strongly, determined to win the debate at all costs, and treated the other person like an adversary. Secondly, she never expressed what she was feeling, but always acted as though she was successful in everything she did, so that people who met her sometimes commented afterward that they found her a bit cold. Pearl would have said that she hated to feel vulnerable, so didn't want to show her weakness to others. But that lack of expression of feeling cut her off from people she wanted to draw close to.

Often shyness prevents people from expressing their feelings to others, and that fear increases in the very situations where they most want connection. When you fear that showing some part of yourself will cut off connection, you actually achieve through concealment the very thing you fear. Fortunately, the opposite is also true: when you allow yourself to be vulnerable by showing your feelings, the removal of your mask allows people to get to know the real you. Your expression of truth brings you closer to other people.

 Spend a day becoming more aware of the language you hear and use.

1. Listen out for the words, "I feel" from other people, and note the context, and the impact they have.
2. (Harder to spot) Notice how many times you yourself say "I feel"– "I feel worried, I feel relieved, I feel upset, I feel excited". Note also that the word "feel" is sometimes understood but not actually said – e.g. "I'm worried", "I'm excited".
3. Deliberately use the words, "I feel" in a conversation in an appropriate context, and notice its impact and your reaction to using it.

 Note that "I feel *that*" doesn't count as Heart Talk, as that phrase introduces an opinion, not a feeling. For example, "I feel *that* we're running late" or "I feel *that* you ought to apologize to your partner."

Look at the Heart Talk questions earlier in this chapter, and see how you might adapt them in conversation to increase connection with someone. Here are a few more openings to guide you. Try them out.

- What do you enjoy/love about . . .?
- Why do you like/love/enjoy . . .?
- Why/how is . . . important to you?
- What matters to you about . . .?
- What does . . . mean for you?
- How do you feel when . . .?
- What do you feel about . . .?

When you want to connect with someone on this level, it's all about *how* you speak. If you ask the questions above in a clipped and business-like tone, you'll get Head Talk or Action Talk in return. If you ask as if you care, the other person is more likely to open up to you with Heart Talk.

Be especially aware of your voice tone when you start a question with "why". Use the word with gentle curiosity, otherwise you sound like an inquisitor!

RISK TAKING

There is a risk in sharing your innermost thoughts and feelings with other people. What if they should misunderstand, or scorn you or – heaven forbid – laugh at you? T. S. Eliot's Prufrock dreads to speak to a woman of love: "Do I dare?" he asks himself, "Do I dare?" What if he were to read love in a woman's behaviour and she should respond, "That is not what I meant at all; That is not it, at all." What loss of face and embarrassment! But isn't there a bigger risk in losing out on real connection and closeness with others through closing off your feelings? The great thing about conversation is that you can go step by step, testing the waters as you go – a small feeling statement here, a minor revelation there, and carry on only as trust builds between you.

There is nothing more powerful than emotional truth in building connection, and people are most influenced through feelings. When we hide emotion, we hide access to this influence. We talk about telling the truth, but emotional truth is more profound and more powerful than factual truth.

7.5 Soul talk

"The natural voice is transparent – revealing, not describing, inner impulses of emotion and thought, directly and spontaneously."
– Kirsten Linklater

Have you ever had the heart-warming experience of talking to someone and feeling accepted and understood, and therefore able to be yourself – indeed, able to *discover* more who you truly are?

SEEING SOMEONE FOR WHO THEY REALLY ARE

Soul talk becomes possible when you are fully present and experiencing what is happening in the here and now. Too often we are disconnected from our current experience – dwelling on the past or worrying about the future. We experience the magic of soul connection when we are fully present and "see" each other in the full sense of the term.

Through *being seen* in conversation we learn about ourselves, and gain confidence in who we are. Everything about us flourishes when we are truly seen by another human being. Even if you are habitually self-critical and don't view yourself very positively, when you speak with someone who looks beneath the surface and sees the core of possibility in you, you begin to see what they see and start to feel good about yourself. You gain confidence that while remaining authentic you can relate to people and gain their trust.

When you converse with someone on this level, you connect with them beyond what they think, feel and do, often beyond the actual words you use. But, using words, you can ask questions that speak to the person's sense of inner-being:

- Who are you at your best?
- How is writing part of who you are?
- What is your sense of yourself when you're playing the piano?
- Who do you sense you are when you're engaged in doing what you love to do?

All these questions are versions of "who are you?" and if you are to answer them authentically, your reply will always have the sense of being, "I am . . ." – "I am at peace"; "I am fulfilled"; "I am a guide"; "This *is* me."

I was chatting to a friend who loves mountain climbing, and as he spoke about his experiences, I understood that here was an activity where he truly found himself. So I asked him lightly, "Who are you when you're up there in the mountains?" and he replied:

It's a testing environment, and I feel scared at times, but there's nowhere else I feel so much myself – so alive, so connected to nature – connected to everything. It's just me and the mountain, and every cell in my body is vibrantly alive. That's the real me, I guess! You know, free, brave, joyful . . .!

I felt privileged to share that intimate revelation.

Other people find it hard to find words for such experiences. Some will come up with a simile or metaphor to express what they are trying to say.

Carmen was explaining how she had found her vocation in teaching: "Teaching's what I was born to do," she said.

"Who do you feel you are as a teacher?" I asked.

She replied, "Who? That's an odd question. I suppose I see myself as a kind of magnet, attracting the children towards exciting discoveries. Not forcing them, or making them do stuff – rather drawing them in by making things fascinating. Yes, a magnet, that's me!"

 People come up with amazing metaphors sometimes. A business coach who participated in one of my courses suddenly had the image of the yellow Teletubby Laa-Laa in the British television programme for pre-schoolers. In the programme Laa-Laa likes to sing and dance, and is caring too. The trainer laughed with surprise when the image suddenly popped into her mind. But she found that it was spot on. The image expressed the lightness and fun that she brings to her clients in a job she cares deeply about and takes utterly seriously. Every time she thought of the image of Laa-Laa she felt a rush of energy and enjoyment that she recognized as the best of her.

Sometimes when we know someone really well, we stop truly seeing them, and instead see only our partial habitual version of who they are. Someone I was coaching confessed to me once, "The one place I don't have conversations is in my family. My kids don't talk to me, and my wife talks but says nothing." They ended up with empty conversations that they both interpreted in habitual stereotypical fashion without really seeing each other:

WIFE: *I thought we might go shopping on Saturday.*
(Interpreted by the husband as her stock "let's spend your money" conversation.)

HUSBAND: *I had a hard day today.*
(Interpreted by the wife as his stock "you don't work as hard as I do" conversation.)

SON: *I'm going out.*
(Interpreted by both husband and wife as the typical "escaping from responsibility as usual" conversation.)

Seeing always requires us to see afresh as if for the first time.

Next time you are in conversation with someone you know well, imagine that you are meeting them for the first time and notice details you are not usually aware of. Pay exquisite attention to everything:

- Their appearance.
- Their movement and gestures, their body balance.
- Subtle changes in their mouth and skin.
- Their eyes – look deep into their eyes.
- The form of words they use.
- Their tone of voice.

Every time you find yourself drawing a habitual conclusion or thinking a habitual thought, question yourself, "Is that *really* true? How else might I see this?"

COMMUNICATION BEYOND WORDS

In intimate conversations, when people are in love or when there is a deep bond, communication always goes beyond the actual words spoken. The content of the conversation can even be inconsequential while the underlying meaning is immense. A person's intention and meaning is to be discovered in their cadences, their flowing or staccato rhythms and pregnant silences – meaning flowing beneath the surface of the conversation like a great secret river.

> The other day, I had to wait for a long time with a relative in a hospital outpatients' department. The department was busy, and just opposite us a poorly dressed middle-aged woman was sitting in the next seat to a formally dressed old lady. The old lady looked tense and highly anxious. I didn't get the impression that they were together. But every now and then, the younger woman made a comment to the old lady in an accent I thought might be Polish. Eventually, the old lady responded to these overtures and they fell into conversation about this and that. It was clear that the Polish woman understood the other woman's fear, and was extending the hand of friendship. Her words were simply a melody; the meaning was in her looks and body language that said, "I see you and understand your loneliness – I'm with you in this moment." Her conversation visibly affected the old lady, who gradually relaxed and became calmer and happier.

Patricia Salwei writes about such moments where the real conversation runs beneath the surface:

We sit across from one another
and speak
of trivial matters;
   of the weather
   of your heartbreak
   of your new cobalt scarf.
– from *When the Gods and Goddesses Enter* by Patricia Salwei

In her poem, she describes how she touches the threads of the scarf to get closer to the other person in this time of heartbreak, and in the silence that follows their mask slips away and they find the truth.

A hospice carer told me of similar intimate conversations at the bed of a dying person – full of pauses and silences, but where the connection is transparent and true between carer and patient. The poet Rumi suggests that words are often just a pretext. "It is the inner bond that draws one person to another, not words."

Often the deepest connection happens in the silences. Cicero claimed that silence was one of the great arts of conversation. Just as a great artist is as interested in the spaces between objects as in the objects themselves, so in some conversations the silence between the words conveys more than any speech.

Soul Talk sometimes happens surprisingly easily between strangers. For some people it can feel safer to open up to an understanding stranger they'll never see again than to someone who knows them well. The writer Peter Hessler tells of some of the intimate revelations he has heard from strangers during casual conversations in a bar. One man confessed within five minutes of striking up conversation that he'd just been released from prison; another told him his wife had just died and he hoped to die himself very soon.

Moments of intimacy are possible anywhere when you look beneath the surface.

GENERATIVE CONVERSATIONS

"The meeting of two personalities is like the contact of two chemical substances: if there is any reaction both are transformed."
– Albert Einstein

When two people have reached this level of connection with each other, the possibilities are rich. It's as if, having seeing who you are, the other person then begins to intuit who you *can be*, and you both get a sense of larger possibilities and potential.

In this connected space, you move from "I" and "you" to a sense of "we". You find yourselves understanding each other's intention, and experience an elation that comes from the sympathetic vibrations between you.

In this space you can explore fundamental questions about life and its meaning, not in the sense of exchanging opinions or stating fixed ideas, but with a mutual acceptance of uncertainty and paradox, and the possibility of holding on to different realities and possibilities and different levels of meaning at the same time.

In such conversations you both delight in not knowing and dance in the moment. It becomes possible to ask deep or spiritual questions without any sense of awkwardness or irony. You're able to generate larger connections and deeper meanings beyond a single person, and create something more than the sum of your parts.

Now this may sound like a once in a lifetime conversation, but whenever we open ourselves to another person, whether romantically or in collaboration or friendship, we can both give and learn and make a difference – even create something important together. When two people meet in this way, they don't just exchange facts and opinions; they influence each other's thoughts and create new ones together. Influence works in both directions, and both come away transformed.

Moreover, in creating a strong connection, it's as if we gain access to a deeper source of human thinking. Einstein stressed that humans are part of something bigger, "the whole called by us universe", though they experience themselves as separate. "The most beautiful thing we can experience is the mysterious," he said. "It is the source of all true art and science." Jung describes a layer of the unconscious mind where a man's mind widens out and merges into the unconscious mind of mankind, a level where "we are no longer separate individuals, we are all one". When two minds come together on this level, miracles happen.

7.6 Progressing through talk-types

In the normal flow of a conversation, you will naturally step in and out of different kinds of talk. If you want to connect better with someone – become more intimate, improve a relationship, make a new friend or gain better mutual understanding – you can steer your way purposefully through different talk-types to achieve your intention. If at any stage the other person fails to respond to your subtle invitation to move to a different kind of talk, you can gracefully stay with your current type of conversation, or try something different. You can move through different talk-types surprisingly quickly when you want to, even with a stranger, though your progress will depend on the response you get at each step of the way.

Here's an abbreviated conversation in a work context showing how you can move through talk types to become more closely connected to someone. Both speakers engage in taking the conversation to a deeper level.

Hello, I'm Sasha, have you been here before? (Thing Talk)
No, it's my first time. Pretty crowded, isn't it? (Thing Talk) *What do you do?* (Action Talk)
I'm an environmental engineer. We're currently working on a large building project in Dover, but have to translocate some great crested newts before the building can even start. Fun job! (Action Talk – hint of Heart Talk at the end)
Wow, I didn't realize great crested newts were important! How do you go about it? (Head Talk)
Good question! Well, it's about understanding exactly what they need to thrive, so that when they're moved, they do well in the new location. (Head Talk) I enjoy it actually – it's subtler than it seems to keep great crested newts happy! (Heart Talk)

What do you enjoy about it? (Heart Talk)

Well, these creatures are seemingly not very important, but they're rare, so they matter. I like to feel that I'm the person to rescue them – I'm saving the planet by caring about the little critters, if you like! (Soul Talk)

The world's an amazing place . . . And you're right – it's often small things that matter most – I find that too. (Soul Talk)

Unlike this discussion, many conversations jump about with people responding at different levels.

 Have a go at detecting what's happening in terms of type-talk here:

1. "How do you feel about having to move to London just when you've settled here?"
   - *"London offers huge opportunities in terms of shopping and entertainment."*
2. "What do you do at weekends?"
   - *"Dancing! I absolutely adore it. I never feel more myself than when I'm moving to a strong beat!"*
3. "How have you been?"
   - *"I tidied up the kitchen cupboard today – the ants have got in again."*
4. "What do you think about the conflict in the Middle East?"
   - *"It troubles me deeply, and it makes me realize that going out to help in war-stricken countries is my mission in life."*

Here are the answers:

1. Heart Talk question; Thing Talk answer.
2. Action Talk question; Heart Talk and Soul Talk answer.

---

3. Heart Talk question; Action Talk and Thing Talk answer.
4. Head Talk question; Heart Talk and Soul Talk answer.

The more you can become familiar with talk types, the more easily you will flow purposefully between them, and influence the direction of your conversations.

☞ Sometime when you're in a meeting or in a group of friends, step out mentally for a few minutes and spend some time listening to the conversation.

- Distinguish the different kinds of talk.
- Notice how some people restrict themselves to very few types of talk and how that affects the conversation.
- Notice any obvious mismatches – when, for example, one person confines their talk entirely to action, whilst the other person always expresses feelings.
- Notice which remarks increase connection and which don't.

Don't worry if you struggle to categorize every type of talk accurately. The main thing is to notice how different ways of speaking create different effects, and help or hinder a conversation.

Voice tone and body language are great tools for moving from one type of talk to another. You can use them subtly to invite the other person to enter a different territory without giving a lead as strong as actually saying something in words, and the other person can accept or not. If you speak about a subject in a "no-nonsense" voice, the other person knows that you are engaged in Head or Action Talk. If you ask a question speaking with feeling from the heart, the other person is likely to engage their feelings. You know the other person has responded to the invitation if they follow your lead. If they don't follow, the relationship is not harmed, you just continue on the current track.

☞ Use your voice and body language to say the words, "What's that about?" in different ways, and notice their different effects. Imagine that a friend tells you they are feeling stuck at work.

I'm really stuck at the moment.
What's that about?
(Firm voice and gesture invites the speaker to focus on practical causes and action.)
What's that about?
(Lower empathetic voice and open body language invites the speaker to express her feelings.)
What's that about?
(Gentle high voice expressed with genuine lightness and ease encourages openness and transparency.)
What's that about?
(Slow words from a place deep within encourages the other person to search deep within.)

In the next chapter, I look more closely at such uses of voice and body language to convey your meaning.

8

EXPRESSING YOURSELF

"If you want the truth,
I'll tell you the truth:
Listen to the secret sound,
the real sound,
which is inside you."
– Kabir

I've heard people declare, "I mean what I say and I say what I mean".

If only it were that simple! What if I were to take you by the shoulders, shake you and yell, "I love you!" How would you interpret those words? Or if I folded my arms, tightened my jaw and said in a high clipped voice, "No, I don't mind! I don't mind at all!" Would you take my words at face value?

> *How* you say what you say has a significant impact on how other people interpret it – quite apart from the actual words you use. People always make meaning of your expression and body language.

You hear people lament sometimes, "But I told him I wasn't upset!" sounding deeply hurt even as they say the words. The words are the surface structure, and the meaning is a much less obvious deep structure. Being hidden under the surface language, the meaning of what you say has to be "interpreted" by the listener via your expression, breathing, tone of voice, body language, pauses, and a host of tiny clues. Words don't have fixed meanings.

So when you think about expressing yourself in a conversation, you need to take into consideration various different factors beyond the actual words you say; and the first of these is the sound of your voice.

8.1 Expressing you – voice

"There is no index of character so sure as the voice."
– Benjamin Disraeli

BE HEARD AND UNDERSTOOD

The first possible misunderstanding in conversation is thinking that in saying the words you have communicated with the other person. You haven't communicated anything unless they've heard and grasped what you're saying. People don't always let us know if they haven't quite caught our words, and if the effort to understand is too great, people just give up.

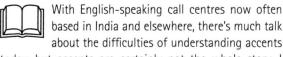 With English-speaking call centres now often based in India and elsewhere, there's much talk about the difficulties of understanding accents today, but accents are certainly not the whole story. I couldn't understand a coachee who came from Aberdeen in Scotland, and constantly asked him to repeat himself. Eventually, he shrugged his shoulders and said, "It's my accent, isn't it? You need to learn Scottish!" His accent was strong, but that wasn't the main problem. He also talked very fast, didn't open his mouth and constantly mumbled and hesitated. So we worked on those issues. When he slowed down, articulated better and varied his delivery, I could understand him perfectly well, and enjoyed his accent.

You can find much more about how to speak clearly in my book, *Voice and Speaking Skills For Dummies.*

So the first voice principle is to be understood. Here are some basics to help you:

- Speak at a steady pace. Slow down even more if your accent is unfamiliar to your listener.
- Take good breaths to power your words and give them flow.
- Relax – your voice will work much better if you're not tense.
- Open your mouth when you speak. Articulate the consonants clearly, and shape the vowels. Especially enjoy long consonants, as in *mmagic* and *wwonderful*; and long vowels, as in *vaast* and *cooool*.
- Emphasize the most important words in each sentence – the ones that really **matter** to the **sense**.
- Vary your pitch. It's much more difficult to understand the meaning if every word has the same emphasis and tone. It's boring too.

SPEAK WITH FLOW

> If you fear that you are not articulate, practise speaking in whole sentences and expressing your ideas clearly.
>
> To get used to a flow of words in everyday life, practise answering with more than a simple yes or no when people ask questions. Get used to making a sentence each time. Here is an example with three possible answers that are all more than just yes or no.
>
> Do you like fish?
> *Yes, I do.*
> *Yes, I love every kind of fish.*
> *No, I'm not very fond of fish, to be honest.*

To make a conversation flow, try adding a question back to the other person as part of your answer:

Do you like fish?
Yes, I do. I think I prefer it to meat. What about you?
Are you speaking at the meeting?
Yes, I'm speaking about the Africa Project. You were involved in organizing the finance for that, weren't you?

 If you find that you tend to hesitate and stumble when you speak, practise the following:

1. Ask yourself a question (or get a friend to ask you); for example, "Explain your work role to me", or "What have you organized for your holiday this year?"
2. Answer the question out loud. It doesn't matter if you hesitate or ramble a bit – this is your first reply.
3. Now ask yourself, "What were my main points?" Marshall your thoughts and give a second answer, shorter than the first one.
4. Ask yourself again, "What's my main thrust?" This time make your answer even shorter and more to the point than before.

Gradually, you will find you get used to organizing your thoughts before you speak, to achieve greater eloquence and flow. This is a useful exercise not only for conversation, but also for interviews, speaking in meetings and any occasion where you are called upon to express yourself without preparation.

GETTING RID OF USELESS FILLERS

Some of us pepper our conversation with little filler words and sounds like, you know, sort of, erm, well, what I'm trying to say is, um, you see, er . . . They can be persistent, and it's quite difficult to eliminate them if you just try *consciously* to cut them out of your speech, as they slip in even before you're aware of them. By focusing on other relevant elements of your speech the fillers will disappear on their own. For example:

- Give yourself space to think before you reply. *A thinking pause is good!* Many people stumble because they rush into words before they're ready.
- Take a deliberate full breath before each thought. Many filler sounds slip in when you run out of air and take an extra snatched breath halfway through a sentence.
- Use your air freely as you speak – don't hold it back to make it last longer. Take a proper breath each time and breathe where you need to. Using lots of air gives your speech energy and direction.
- Once again, slow down! This steadies your mind and gives it longer to formulate what you want to say.
- The more comfortable you are in your own shoes, the easier you will find it to be fluent. So relax, chill and give yourself a pat on the back to encourage yourself every time you manage a fluent sentence!

EXPRESSING INTEREST AND SOUNDING INTERESTING

Your voice has a much bigger role than merely shaping the words you want to say – its tone can express interest, passion, determination, excitement, uncertainty, caring and much more. It has enormous potential to express what you really intend and feel and to bring life to a conversation.

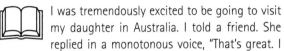I was tremendously excited to be going to visit my daughter in Australia. I told a friend. She replied in a monotonous voice, "That's great. I hope you have a good time." I quickly passed on to other things, feeling unheard. Later, I told another friend my news. Her voice rose in enthusiasm. "Oh, that's so exciting for you! That's great. When do you go? I bet you can't wait!" And through the liveliness and energy of her sound, I felt truly heard.

This is where little words come into their own. When I heard my friend's high pitched, "Oh", I heard that she shared my excitement. "Ooh" in "Ooh, I've just remembered something" gives a sense of urgency to the statement. "No!" in response to surprising negative news shares the speaker's emotion without taking over the conversation yourself.

You may have one tone of voice that you use for everything. It will greatly help you connect in conversation if you are able to vary your voice according to what you are thinking and feeling. This is partly about learning how to use your voice in different ways – maybe from a voice coach or a course on voice – and partly about allowing yourself to take a risk and be more open, so that others can see and hear what is actually going on for you – your pleasure, anger, determination, passion and joy.

It's good to remember that people can only connect with what they see, hear and feel – in other words they only have externals to go on. They are not inside your head and heart. So when, for example, someone hears your voice, they interpret your message *through* your voice, whatever words you use. If you say, "I care about you!" in a sharp voice, they interpret "sharp" and feel uncared for. If you say, "I want you to stop that immediately" in a high wavering voice, they interpret "wavering" and don't take much notice. The Persian poet, Rumi, talks about "the enormous difference between light and the words that try to say light".

It is so easy to betray meaning even when you don't intend to. I heard a neighbour in the summer holidays ask her teenage daughter: "*Are you going to stick at home or go out and get a job?*" "Stick at home" was spoken in a dull low voice, and then her voice rose to an upbeat "get a job", making it absolutely clear where her own preferences lay.

RAPPORT

Sound is particularly important for building a connection. Many people would say that they notice people's appearance more than their voice tone, but voice impacts strongly beneath conscious awareness. If a business-woman is calm, efficient, smart, emotionally intelligent and has a shrill voice, she probably won't be seen as leadership material because her voice jars with people's idea of leadership. Other reasons may well be given for the judgement, but her voice is key. Someone who mumbles is usually considered weak. You can be wonderfully empathetic, but if your voice is harsh, most people won't consider you so.

> The ability to adjust your voice subtly to tune into another person gives them a sense of connection with you more than almost any other factor. It's well worth working on your voice to give yourself more flexibility and variety in how you speak to people.

8.2   Expressing you – body language

"She let her walking do her talking,
She's a brilliant conversationalist."
– T. Graham Brown, lyrics to *Brilliant Conversationalist*

You don't need expansive gestures to converse, and in many cultures – China and Japan, for instance – people gesture little. But that does not mean that the body is not intimately involved in communication. Every actor knows that you use your whole body to express yourself, from the look in your eyes to the position of your feet. Everything about you says something:

- Your posture suggests confidence and ease, openness and stillness – or the opposite. The balance of your body shows how grounded and calm you are.
- Gestures underline the sense of your words, support the voice and help you to explain abstract concepts. According to research by the psychologist Jana Iverson, they even help you to think.
- You move more when you get animated and become still in quieter calmer moments.
- Your breathing changes with your mood, faster for heightened emotion, slower for calmer moments.
- Your eyes speak volumes – friendship, trust, fun, humour, seriousness, sadness, wisdom – they are truly the windows of the soul.
- Your face expresses your thoughts and emotions as you frown, raise an eyebrow, tighten your lips, stiffen your jaw, soften your look or smile radiantly.
- Your skin colour may change as your state of mind changes – from pale when you are detached to coloured when you are emotional or embarrassed.

Give your body language a workout. Imagine you have lost your voice temporarily, and need to communicate some information. Imagine how you would do this without your voice, using just your body – posture, gestures, movement, breathing, eye movements and facial expressions as described previously. Think up your own scene, or try one of these – all in silence!

- You explain to the waiter that your coffee is cold and you'd like it replaced with a hot cup.
- You thank your host warmly for his hospitality, and explain that you can't say it in words as you've lost your voice.
- As someone steps into the room you tell them in no uncertain terms that they cannot come in and that this room is private.

In this exercise, most people are aware initially of the gestures and facial expressions they make in the effort to be understood. But notice too how much you use feelings and movements inside your body to convey your meaning. You won't feel as much movement as this when you use your voice as well, but if you normally keep your body still, reflect on how much more you might use your body to add to your meaning.

Your body is always highly involved in your communication, even though sometimes the movements may be imperceptible.

You might think that body language is for the speaker to think about rather than the listener. But as a listener too, your body movements are vital to show the speaker that you are listening and understanding. The movements can be small, but without them the speaker will probably feel as if they are speaking into a vacuum. When you feel connected to the other person and relax, you move naturally.

 Notice these and similar movements when you listen:

- Your head leaning a little as you listen.
- Nodding your head very slightly to show you agree or understand.
- Shaking your head slowly in sympathy.
- Smiling at times in encouragement.
- Using your eyes and facial muscles to respond to what you are hearing.
- Changes in your breathing as you respond in different ways.

8.3   Expressing you – your emotions

*"There can be no transforming of darkness into light or apathy
into movement without emotion."*
– Carl Jung

Voice tone and body language are the outward and visible signs
of your inner energy, which is fuelled by your emotions. Emotions
play an important part in conveying your meaning to the other
person. If you keep your emotions locked away, you make it much
more difficult for the other person to understand you. Yet many
of us are so used to hiding our emotions that we do it instinc-
tively, and so create a distance between ourselves and other
people.

INFLUENCING WITH YOUR EMOTIONS

Emotions are highly influential. Once both of you are at ease in
conversing with each other, emotions become "sticky", and the
other person catches your emotional energy. If you become passionate, the other person catches your passion. Your joy makes
them joyful, your excitement energizes them and your stillness
calms them. This is exactly how you inspire others – through
feelings.

This only happens, though, if you genuinely feel those emotions
yourself *and* allow the other person to witness you feeling them.
And here's the rub. For many of us, we have to feel very comfortable with another person before we allow them to see our
emotions. Otherwise we feel vulnerable and the risk seems too
great.

An intelligent awareness of emotions is extremely useful in conversation. Let's look at some of the ways here.

- When you are at ease, you put others at ease. Your emotional calm allows others to find a sense of calm too.
- When you adapt emotionally to what is going on – i.e. show concern when someone is anxious, react in a lively way when someone is excited, and show strength when someone is aggressive – you get onto the other person's wavelength and they feel understood. This helps the conversation to flow.
- When you are able to read a mood, you are able to judge situations better and have more choices in how to respond.

 When you listen, listen to sounds as much as to words. Not everyone expresses emotion in the words they use.

 The journalist Tim Dowling writes of taking a photo of his 18-year-old son all dressed up for the first time in black jacket and tie ready for his school leaving party. He takes the shot in the very same spot where his son had posed in his new uniform on his first day of primary school, years before. Tim lines it all up, and his throat closes with emotion without warning. He blinks several times to get his swimming vision to hold still. "I'd better do another one," he says. The words tell you nothing, but every parent of an 18-year-old would hear in the choked sound all the brimming emotions of the parent of a child on the cusp of adulthood. (*The Guardian Weekend*, 13 July 2013)

8.4   Expressing the real you

"Whatsoever you do, if you can do it with your total presence, your life will become ecstatic; it will be a bliss."
– Osho

Connection at a deeper level happens when both people are authentic. To connect closely with someone they need to see you as you truly are, not as someone you are not.

 The greatest gift you can bring to a conversation is yourself. This is the most important and probably the scariest thing for you to know.

If you feel anxious or critical or not good enough, you pretend, thinking it won't be noticed. But pretence puts up a barrier between you and other people, and they notice that something's amiss. Your thoughts produce feelings; feelings leak out into voice and body language, and people pick it up.

Being yourself is not the same as *selling* yourself. Some presentation gurus recommend high-octane self-presentation of an image of power whenever you communicate. Though it's good to feel alive, presentation that is obviously a performance often creates resistance in listeners.

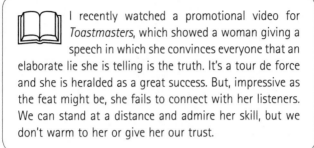

I recently watched a promotional video for *Toastmasters*, which showed a woman giving a speech in which she convinces everyone that an elaborate lie she is telling is the truth. It's a tour de force and she is heralded as a great success. But, impressive as the feat might be, she fails to connect with her listeners. We can stand at a distance and admire her skill, but we don't warm to her or give her our trust.

If you have the courage to be imperfect, you give others permission to make mistakes too, and then you can both be at ease. Letting go of who you think you *should* be, you open the way for kindness to yourself and others and they connect with the real you without your mask. It means not numbing yourself against the bad, but staying aware, sensitive, open to feeling, even if you find yourself blushing with self-consciousness or trembling with fear. If vulnerability frightens you, know that it frightens everyone. Keep breathing and let time flow on. You are most powerful and most alive when you are yourself. Being yourself you can connect in conversation with *anybody*. You can step into the unknown, and enjoy the wonder of discovery with another human being.

Part Three

Sailing Through Tricky Waters

"Pray don't talk to me about the weather, Mr Worthing. Whenever people talk to me about the weather, I always feel quite certain that they mean something else. And that makes me quite nervous."

– Oscar Wilde

Sometimes the going gets tough. A conversation gets confusing or stuck, or you don't like the direction it's taking. You feel you're not dealing with a real person or you suspect that they're playing games with you. The other party gets difficult and you encounter conflict. In this chapter, I look at some of the ways you can deal with problematic conversations.

WHAT TO DO IF YOU'RE STUCK

9.1   Find a positive state of mind

 Maurice's senior manager walked up to him at the conference and asked him how things were going.

"Fine," answered Maurice, slightly embarrassed.

"Good, good, that's good," muttered his manager after a short pause. "Everything's okay then?"

"Er, yes, yes, it's all going well, thanks," stuttered Maurice.

"That's good then, that's good," replied his manager, and he shuffled off.

Afterwards, Maurice exploded to his friend. "Honestly, what on earth was I meant to say? I felt so stupid! He just stood there and didn't say anything."

What *do* you do when the conversation splutters and dies or never actually gets going?

- Remember that your brain is affected by how you feel. Maurice let himself feel intimidated. Keep breathing, it'll help you think; and encourage yourself by remembering times when you have felt good and been in control.

- Remind yourself of equality in conversation. If you have internal blocks such as "He's senior to me, it's his call," or "He's going to think me stupid," you'll feel daunted. Reassure yourself that you are an equal partner at this moment.

- Remember that any simple question or remark can move the conversation forward – for example, "How are you finding the conference?" or even a weather remark: "Great day for the conference isn't it?" or "Good to be inside on a rainy day like this, isn't it?"

9.2 Stop faking it

Sometimes people get stuck because they decide to hide their ignorance and then can't keep up the pretence.

 Jake was talking to a client:

CLIENT: *Of course, we're now using tele-presence videoconferencing – so much more sophisticated.*

JAKE: Yes, it's definitely superior, isn't it? (Thinks: *What on earth is it?*)

CLIENT: *Which system do you favour?*

JAKE: Well, I er, we er, . . .

So you're stuck. It's better to use the *confident ignorance* strategy – that is, to reveal that you don't know but without being apologetic about it. For instance, "Tele-presence? That's new, isn't it? How are you finding it?"

9.3 Slow down

At the other end of the spectrum from the awkward silence lies an equally disabling inability to *stop* talking – you start wittering and your words run away completely out of control. The tendency to witter comes from nervous tension – just as silence does. In this case, instead of shutting down your brain's ability to think, the anxiety shuts down your ability to listen. So, to avoid those gaps where you might be expected to listen, your subconscious rushes you forward and your words tumble over each other.

 If you have this tendency, then catch the following habit: "Stop, breathe, speak low and slow":

1. As soon as you start to rush, say firmly to yourself "Stop!"
2. Then relax your shoulders and body and take a good breath.
3. Then slow down and speak with a deeper voice.

When you do this, you become calmer and your ability to listen improves.

9.4 Know the rules of the game

Sometimes a conversation doesn't work very well because the other person plays by different rules than you. The answer is often then to join them in their game!

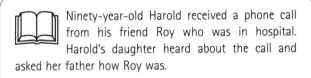 Ninety-year-old Harold received a phone call from his friend Roy who was in hospital. Harold's daughter heard about the call and asked her father how Roy was.

"He didn't tell me," replied Harold.
"Well, didn't you ask him?" enquired his daughter.
"No, I didn't like to pry," responded Harold. "He'd have told me if he wanted me to know."

His unspoken rule was that you don't ask questions. If you waited to be asked a question to tell him something, you'd wait forever!

Harold's son-in-law was fed-up with being "talked at" every time he met his father-in-law. So he tried breaking in with his own subjects, and was pleasantly surprised to find that Harold was very happy to listen. He'd assumed that Harold had no interest in other people, when in fact he was just reticent about asking questions.

Some people ask questions, some don't; some dislike being interrupted while others expect it and enjoy the energy of mutual interrupting. Judge the moment; be attentive to the other person's reaction and find out what works.

9.5 Being flexible

Flexibility is exactly what you need when a conversation becomes difficult. Basically, if it's not working, do something different!

- If your contributions to a conversation are always statements, try a question instead. If you mostly find yourself asking questions of the other person, practise creating statements instead.
- The more you can adjust your behaviour without losing your sense of who you are, the better you make a connection, even in trickier circumstances. If you can speak tough to match toughness, and gentle to match gentleness at the appropriate time, the other person will feel you've got the measure of them and be easier to deal with.
- If you encounter difficulties, you might like to imagine yourself in a different role from the one you actually hold. If you want to stand up to a strong personality for instance, imagine yourself in a more senior position and speak and act accordingly.

 Neville was generally a kind and mild-mannered man, and people were surprised that he seemed more successful than his colleagues at standing up to a domineering boss. One day I asked him, "How do you do it? You don't seem domineering, yet the boss listens to you." "I'll tell you," he said "and don't laugh. It's very simple. I just imagine that I'm a lion whenever I go into his office. I saw some incredible animals out in the Masai Mara – they're still and powerful – and I just get a sense of that before I go into our boss's den." He smiled. "But I wouldn't want everyone to know that." I promised to keep his secret (and I've changed his name!).

OILING THE WHEELS

Sometimes, you're not completely stuck in a conversation, but it's not really flowing either and you need some back-up tools. So here are a few to try:

10.1 Comment on what you've already heard

You can hark back to the other person's previous statement and make a comment about it to show that you are still interested.

 Stephanie was telling Kevin about her safari trip to Tanzania. She came to a pause, and concluded, "So all in all we had a great time." There followed a silence that seemed to go on a bit too long. So Kevin made a general comment on what Stephanie had said so far to prompt her:

Sounds as if it was one of your best trips ever?

Stephanie replied, "Oh, yes it was!" and immediately thought of something else she wanted to say about the trip.

Kevin could also have asked a question about a previous comment to elicit more detail:

What was it like, being so close to the animals?
Tell me, what was it like, camping out in the wild?

Imagine for yourself various questions you could ask. The same openings can be used in many different contexts:

- What's it like? What was it like when you . . .?
- Tell me about it? Tell me about . . .
- How is it? How was it?
- How did it feel, when you . . .?

Prompting is especially useful if the other person is struggling to articulate what they'd like to say. It shows your interest, and often triggers interesting fresh information even after they appear to have finished.

10.2 Encouraging nods and grunts

Sometimes a conversation falters because of lack of positive feedback. I coached a team leader who hated conference calls because they meant she had to speak into a void without the feedback of seeing anyone's response as she spoke. Most people find it much easier to speak if they know that the other person is attending to what they have to say.

A face-to-face conversation can feel like talking into a vacuum if the other person fails to give signals that they have heard you. If I announce to someone that I'm thrilled to have just won a competition, I appreciate some little noise to show that the other person has heard and noted my comment. Just a brief "Oh great!" or "Good!" will do – or even a cheerful grunt! It's surprising how encouraging non-verbal sounds can be in showing speakers that they're being listened to and understood. Try "yeh?", "uh-huh", "oh", "mmm" and "yay!" – all gold-dust noises! Body language – a smile or nod – works well too. Turning or looking away has the opposite effect, even if you are listening well.

11

ROLE PLAYING

We all behave differently with different people. You may play mad games with your children and suffer their jokes at your expense first thing in the morning, and then later stride confidently into the office as a powerful determined executive and play that role until the end of the working day. But if you stick to a limited role and leave too much of the real you at home, you severely limit the possibilities in your interactions and things get stuck.

Jack, head of an engineering company, lived quite a chaotic and unsatisfying personal life. He didn't believe in bringing his home self into the office, and thought it nobody's business what he did outside work. His employees knew little about him. He, in turn, was not interested in their lives, and didn't encourage casual chat in the office. His conversations were always focused on the task in hand – and never on his relationship with the person he was talking to. His team thought that in many ways he was good at his job, but he often encountered problems with staff through failing to understand their motivation or attitude. They found him hard to relate to, because he left so much of himself at the door as he entered his office. Moreover, as he didn't value genuine relationships at work, they felt deep down that he didn't value them.

Playing a role has some advantages in a work environment – relationships appear clear and tidy in their hierarchies and everyone knows where they stand. But the rigid rules crush the possibilities of genuine open conversation and relationships fail to thrive.

 It serves anyone to come out from behind their role and be real, so that genuine connection can take place.

 Greg Dyke, former Director General of the BBC, was immensely popular with staff and inspired fierce loyalty. When he was forced out of the BBC after the Hutton enquiry, thousands of staff paid for an advert in a national newspaper supporting him, and over a 1000 of them sent emails begging him to stay. At his departure, several hundred staff, many of them in tears, turned up to cheer him. Dyke commented after-wards, "I don't think they are protesting. They just want to say they are sad. Leading organisations is all about the relationship between people." A colleague who was a fairly lowly member of Dyke's staff at that time told me that employees loved his open management style. He fre-quently moved around in the organization meeting people, always ready to have a conversation with anybody. She herself had chatted with him and found him interested and engaged. "He treated me as an equal," she said.

Risking the personal provides the way not only to better connection, but also to a whole list of benefits. Chatting to people is a way to keep your ear to the ground, to hear what is going on behind the scenes and pick up the underlying state or culture in a group or company. In casual chat, you pick up important information and new ideas. You learn more about people's talents, potential, experience and skills.

You may wonder whether mild-mannered Laura would cope with more responsibility at work, but hearing how she fought with the authorities to gain a good education for her disabled child, you realize that she has hidden strengths as yet untried in the workplace. When you chat with laid-back Dan at the Christmas party and discover that he's raised thousands in funds for his daughter's riding charity, you recognize there's more to him than meets the eye. At the same time, as employees hear about their leader's humorous struggles with navigation on a boating holiday, they warm to his openness and humility.

Casual, open conversation is great for trust building, and from trust comes loyalty, as my friend Helen confirmed. At one time she had a job working for a boss with whom she had an excellent relationship. He trusted her to work at home when she needed to concentrate for particular projects, and she put in a lot of overtime to do an excellent job. A new manager who followed him chatted with nobody, trusted nobody, and insisted that Helen stay in the office and account for every moment of her time. "I gave up working hard then," Helen confessed. "If he couldn't trust me, he lost my loyalty."

You motivate people by understanding them, and there's nothing like a casual chat for finding out what makes people tick. You can then acknowledge them in the way they like to be acknowledged, and get the best from your relationship. If people chat to each other at work, it brings them together and builds a sense of common purpose.

When you meet people at your most genuine, you find the genuine in them. Cecile is a development and learning manager in a million. Responsible for a large number of employees, she has chatted one-to-one with most of them, and really knows each one and what they need. As a result, her members of staff are working to their full potential, and feel motivated and recognized. Her work is not showy – she just relates to individuals and responds to their needs. But it's transforming her company and producing great results.

12

SPOTTING THE GAMES PEOPLE PLAY

As you connect with someone in conversation your trust in each other gradually develops as the conversation proceeds. However, sometimes people *act* as if they are connecting when they are only pretending, and with this false connection they play all manner of games.

If someone is playing a game with you, you might feel uncomfortable and then attribute the reason to your own failings in conversation. So it's good to be able to recognize when someone is playing a game and have counter-moves ready.

12.1 The status game

Keith Johnstone includes a chapter on status in *Impro*, his book on improvisation for actors. In observing people he noticed how status plays a major part in human conversation and he describes how humans play complex games of one-upmanship that are constantly fluctuating and readjusting.

Someone's status often accords with their role in real life, so you'd expect someone with social prominence, wealth and education to have high status; but it doesn't necessarily work like that. A condescending waiter may at that moment be high status while his customer, an awkward professor, is low status. It is high status to top someone's comment with a superior comment of the "my boat/house/salary's bigger than yours" variety. It's also high status to play "one-downmanship", where you claim that your misfortune is worse than the other person's. For example, "You may have had a hernia operation, but I actually *died* for several seconds on the operating table." Low status is played out in agreeing, paying deference and being subservient to the high status player.

Status games are incredibly common in conversation. Human interaction is seldom neutral in terms of status, and in conversation people constantly adjust their status in relation to each other. Many conversations are subtle power plays with each player jockeying for position whilst attempting to disguise their ploys. Every player is trying to win the game, and that involves creating losers. Such conversations can seem like normal social intercourse, but there's a competitive current constantly running underneath that under a guise of pleasantness can become quite nasty.

You weave intricate webs when you play status games. If you win a point too comprehensively, other people in the conversation may gang together to isolate you, and then you have to make a low status comment to get back in the game again.

Here's a conversation where new acquaintances are discussing holidays.

> ANN: Where did you go this year? We tried Rimini – nice safe beaches for the kids.
> SARAH: *We always go to Greece – the coastline's just stunning, full of beautiful inlets only accessible by boat.*

(Slightly higher status – that "stunning" tops "nice and safe", and "only accessible by boat" sounds superior too.)

> CATHY: Oh, we abandoned Greece a few years ago when we discovered the Maldives – it puts everywhere else completely in the shade! We spend a good part of

every summer there now and just don't bother with Europe any more.

(Too strong higher status.)

ANN: (With a little laugh) Well, we don't all get six weeks holiday to go gallivanting off all over the place – some of us work, you know.

(Blocking the high status.)

SARAH: *Did you know the Maldives are drowning – your hotel will be knee deep in water before long!*

(Supporting the block with a joking put-down.)

Ann and Sara laugh. (Conspiracy against Cathy.)

CATHY: Oh well, I'd never run down the Mediterranean. I've always had a lot of fun in the Med.

(Goes lower status to adjust and re-enter the group.)

Keith Johnstone describes the significance of body language in status games. High status players take up a lot of space, move deliberately and hold strong eye contact. Low status players shrink into a small space; constantly fidget with their hair or face, make small meaningless noises, and glance briefly at you, then glance away.

Some people play the game in an obvious way with big power gestures. Others play a hidden game, with subtle power shifts, in flux all the time. In some small groups, the interplay of shifting status is as complex as a game of chess!

Choose a time when you can observe other people, and notice the status games they play. Look out for the following:

- How body language underlines status and supports status comments.
- How a high status player sometimes drops to a lower status to maintain connection.
- How some couples adopt consistent roles, one high status, the other low.
- How people switch alliances in a group to maintain the balance of the conversation in terms of status.

Once you recognize the game, you'll see it everywhere. And fortunately, once spotted, it loses its hold over you. Instead of getting upset or irritated at a comment, you find yourself nodding internally and thinking, "Oh, that old status game", without being riled by it. Recognizing the game, you can also avoid playing the status the other person expects of you. Every high status player trying to dominate the conversation is looking for a low status player to be subservient. You can reject that role.

12.2   The manipulation game

Sales manuals have always suggested ways to manipulate people through conversation. One of the ways people are manipulated is through their unwillingness to break certain accepted codes of conduct. Some salespeople don't play by the same social rules as the rest of us and exploit people's good will. As soon as you suspect that someone is using a sales technique rather than taking part in a genuine conversation, put up your guard and stop considering the exchange a conversation, because it isn't – it's a sales pitch. The rules are different.

☞ First, practise spotting sales voices on the phone. When you receive a call, see how quickly you can tell if it's a sales pitch. Listen out for an instantly bright, brisk-paced voice right from the start, and regularity in the pitch and pace. Then contrast that with your experience when a friend calls – pay attention to their voice tone, speed and flow – notice how much less regular it is. What else can you notice?

A sales person asks you various questions aiming to lead to a final yes from you. Customers who don't like to be impolite by saying no to every question find themselves cornered into saying yes at the end. To play your side of the game – not to be sold to if you don't want to – you don't need to block with a series of no's and feel impolite doing it. Instead, answer briskly and positively, very happy to agree but never to be convinced. Here's a car salesperson in action:

Have you had your current vehicle for some time?
(Brightly) *Yes I have.*

Have you considered changing it at all?

Oh yes, wouldn't that be nice!

Have you seen our current range of fuel-efficient models with the latest features?

Yes, they're wonderful aren't they? Things are changing so fast!

Could I interest you in a tour of our various new models?

(Brightly) *Absolutely not! But thank you! Cars are completely off my agenda for the foreseeable future. Thank you so much for offering to show me your range. You don't sell Persian rugs do you?*

Agreement without being convinced takes the wind out of their sails. They can't push and persuade if you refuse to play their game. Changing the subject at the end isn't a bad move either!

12.3 Old games

Conversations sometimes get stuck in a groove when two participants play the same tune over and over again. For example, one partner plays bully and the other victim, and time and again, over the years, their conversations slip into that groove:

Aren't you ready yet?
Yes, sorry, I'm almost ready.
Why does it always take you so long, it's ridiculous.
I won't be a minute. Sorry to keep you.
Just get your act together can't you? I'm going without you; I can't be bothered with this.
Oh, please wait.

Or one person always acts helpless, and the other person regularly comes to the rescue.

I just can't manage this anymore. I'm hopeless. (Opening gambit in a familiar whining voice.)
Of course you're not hopeless. Let me do it. (Familiar collusion.)

If the second person stopped colluding in the habitual dance, they might say instead:

Do you have a problem? What would you like me to do about it?

Thus forcing the first person to abandon their whining child role.

The "Yes but" game is a familiar one to a lot of people. A rescuer offers help and advice to a victim, and is continually rebutted by "yes but".

I can't find a job. I've looked everywhere.
Have you tried the Internet?
Yes, but ours is always crashing.
Have you tried down at the library?

Yes, but their opening hours have been restricted with all these government cuts.

What about going to an Internet café?

Yes, but I'm not made of money – have you forgotten I'm out of work?

Usually the questioner just gives up defeated, or makes a summarizing comment about how hard it is to get jobs these days. And the victim has won – again.

Eric Berne describes various such stuck roles in his book *Games People Play*. He suggests that at different times people act like adult, child or parent. To the simple question, "Are you joining us for dinner in town tonight?" one person might answer straightforwardly like an adult: "Yes, I'd like to" or "No, I'm afraid I can't." Another person might act like a child: "Why? Do you think I can't manage on my own?" A third person might act like a parent, treating the other person like a child: "You'd save your money if you ate at home more often."

Many people carry on for years thinking they're having unique conversations when they're playing an old familiar game. The biggest leap to escape from this is to realize you *are* playing a game.

 How can you tell if you're in a role game? Ask yourself:

- Is this familiar – or even boring? Have I been here before?
- How do we get to this point every time? What sets it off?
- What do I say or do that slots me into the familiar role?

Then, think of two or three alternatives to try instead. If you change your behaviour, you'll get a different result.

12.4   Naming the game

Another way to counteract such games is to step outside the matrix and name the game. For example, "I've asked you three questions, and each time you have answered, 'yes, but.'"

I was working on a new initiative with a group of managers I hadn't met before, and whatever subject I introduced they responded with little energy, not pronounced enough for me to call it laziness or rebellion, but not focused or engaged. In the end, I stopped in my tracks and got everyone's attention. "There's something here that I'm not getting," I told them. "What's the elephant in the room?" After a bit of shuffling and muttered *nothings*, one of them spoke up. "We haven't anything against you," she said. "It's just we shouldn't be doing this work. It's being forced on us, and a lot of us a very angry about it." As soon as they were honest with me, we were able to find a way forward.

Naming what you perceive can often unblock a conversation that has got stuck. If one party is hiding a strong emotion, it's often useful to name what you notice without accusation: "I'm aware that you are sounding flat. What's that about?" Or, "I'm feeling stuck in this conversation. Are you feeling that too?"

This can be especially useful if the other person is mocking, belittling, or being cynical or sarcastic. You may try confronting the behaviour and they refuse to be pinned down. "Of course I wasn't being sarcastic – can't you take a joke?" If that happens, name specifically what you perceived: "You did or said specifically this, and I made the following meaning from it. *This* is what is going on."

13

ENJOYING DISAGREEMENT

"There is no conversation more boring than the one where every-body agrees."
– Michel de Montaigne

You may feel that any disagreement in conversation is going to be disagreeable or even dangerous, but conversation devoid of disagreement can be boring and bland. Some of the most lively and enjoyable dialogues can be based on disagreement – my recent chat with Polly for instance:

"I *love* Art Deco," proclaimed Polly enthusiastically.

"You *don't!*" I exclaimed in misbelief. "All that crude colour and cubist look – it has no soul!"

"Soul's exactly what it has got," laughed Polly. "Clarice Cliff's designs just sing! Have you really looked at them?"

"Well, maybe I haven't really *looked* at them!" I admitted. "But give me the fine lines and simple elegance of Japanese pottery every time! Do you know the work of Keiko Matsui? It's glorious! Much better than old Clarice Cliff!"

And so we happily continued.

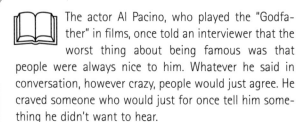

The actor Al Pacino, who played the "Godfather" in films, once told an interviewer that the worst thing about being famous was that people were always nice to him. Whatever he said in conversation, however crazy, people would just agree. He craved someone who would just for once tell him something he didn't want to hear.

But maybe for you the thought of disagreement in conversation creates tension. You fear that if you disagree with someone they'll insult you and create conflict – or that the person will strike back verbally and you'll get upset yourself. Maybe you've had a bad experience of attempting to disagree with someone who then laid into you as if your remark were an invitation to mortal combat. It's certainly true that cultures around the world operate differently when it comes to disagreement, and what is the norm in the US, for instance, might create offence in some Pacific countries. But even if culture is an issue, that doesn't mean that you are condemned always to agree with people – there are ways to disagree that minimize conflict.

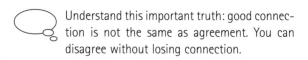

Understand this important truth: good connection is not the same as agreement. You can disagree without losing connection.

We've already discovered that connection depends more on your tone of voice and body language than on the content of your conversation. If you maintain good connection with another person you can say what is true for you and not offend. My conversation about Art Deco with my friend was sparky and fun because we maintained connection and looked at each other and laughed even as we disagreed about the content of our discussion.

> ! The danger is that, feeling awkward about disagreeing, many people disagree both verbally *and* with their voice and body language. They stiffen, fold their arms, hunch over and turn their head away, and then either say nothing or speak in a strained tight voice that breaks all rapport with the other person. Alternatively, they retaliate violently. No wonder they cause a negative reaction!

> ☞ Here's a different tactic. Try this example:
>
> Imagine someone has just told you in an emphatic upbeat voice that Manchester United have the best team ever this season and you strongly disagree.
>
> • Breathe, relax and turn towards them, keeping your body language open and mirroring their energy.
> • Make your voice tone and speed similar to theirs, as you put your own point: "Oh, do you think so? I put my money on Chelsea – a phenomenal team this season!"
>
> So you go with the other person's *energy* (without copying their *mood* if it is negative), and this allows the conversation to flow from one person to the other, even though you are expressing differences.

> 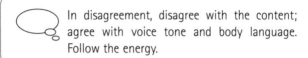 Find an occasion where you can experiment with disagreeing in this way. Most people who try it say that it spices up a conversation and turns it into a genuine discussion as different points of view are aired. Try it out. You'll probably be pleasantly surprised.

> In disagreement, disagree with the content; agree with voice tone and body language. Follow the energy.

By the way, you'll find this skill invaluable in close personal relationships. Any long-standing relationship that never has disagreements is probably stagnating or not as close as it might be. You build closeness in a relationship through disagreeing at times without losing connection. As the poet David Whyte said, "Hey, you can't walk away, I'm angry with you and that means we have a relationship." Conversations that deal with our areas of disagreement help us to be ourselves, to grow and be accountable, and give others the positive message that we think they are strong enough to deal with challenges. That's all great for a relationship.

14

CONFRONTATION

"If you must be candid be candid beautifully."
– Kahlil Gibran

It's one thing to disagree casually in conversation; it's a higher order of challenge to initiate difficult conversations and deliberately confront someone when you need to. You may be tempted to ignore difficulties when you first notice them, but it's easiest to address them before they fester and grow. As you become more skilled in conversation you find that issues that might have been difficult in the past no longer trouble you, as by good listening, showing respect and building connection, you diffuse tricky situations before they have a chance to occur.

Sometimes, however, the situation is too important, the differences too great and the emotions run too strong. Then you need some additional strategies.

The basics remain the same whether you are dealing with minor or major disagreement. You give the other person respect and courtesy by tuning into them with your tone of voice and body language, while you address the content of the difficult issue.

14.1 Handling feelings with skill

If a conversation is confrontational, it's especially important to be comfortable with your own feelings. What looks on the surface like a disagreement over a decision or a point of logic can actually feel like an attack on your sense of self, and the feelings this provokes can be the biggest threat to a positive outcome.

Feelings have a nasty habit of leaking out and becoming visible to the other person, even as you try your hardest to hide them.

- Anger can make you want to put all the problem on the other person and fight, and then you end up accusing and criticizing or insisting and blaming.
- Feeling bad about yourself can make you give up and surrender, or avoid issues.
- Fear can make you freeze emotionally, so you do and say nothing or retreat.

Your feelings can prevent you from focusing and listening properly. Shutting down is no answer, so what can you do?

Focus on yourself for a moment:

- Stay open and real. Keep breathing! Of course you have emotions. You may be feeling fearful, angry, worried or upset. By recognizing those emotions, they lose their power to surprise you.
- As you breathe, realize that there is no need either to be roused to hostility or to appease weakly. You can respond as you wish, and that includes telling the other person what you are feeling without being overwhelmed by the emotion.
- As a strong or violent emotion comes your way, imagine it flowing past you, or flowing through you straight down into the earth without affecting you.

14.2   Checking your assumptions

Your chances of success are significantly increased if you chal-lenge your own negative assumptions beforehand. For example:

- You may assume that there's always a winner and a loser in a confrontation, and therefore do everything you can to win. With this assumption you stride into the conversation with a look that says, "Let the battle commence!" If you do adopt this confrontational stance you'll probably both end up losing.

Think instead in terms of win-win. With skill, you can address the problem as if you're side by side looking at it together. The problem is then neither you nor the other person, but an issue to solve together.

Think ahead of time about what you want from the conversation. Have a vision both of an outcome acceptable to both of you and of a positive future working relationship. Aim for a conversation where you'll look back and be pleased with your behaviour.

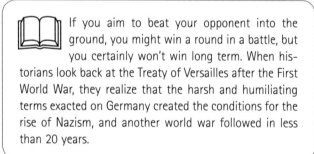

If you aim to beat your opponent into the ground, you might win a round in a battle, but you certainly won't win long term. When his-torians look back at the Treaty of Versailles after the First World War, they realize that the harsh and humiliating terms exacted on Germany created the conditions for the rise of Nazism, and another world war followed in less than 20 years.

- You may assume you're 100% right and the other person 100% wrong. As Harry Wormwood said to Mathilda in Roald Dahl's famous story, "Listen, you little wiseacre: I'm smart, you're dumb; I'm big, you're little; I'm right, you're wrong." And you might add, "I'm good, you're bad; I'm innocent, you're guilty." But things are rarely black and white. With this kind of thinking you assume there'll be opposition from the other side, and treat the other person as an enemy from the start, creating an instant defensive reaction.

You may not be to blame in the least, but still the unique relationship between you and the other person is usually a factor, so recognize that you're involved. If you were someone else it wouldn't be the same; if you acted differently it wouldn't be the same. A conversation of this kind is always a negotiation and the answer is never between black and white, but a different, creative solution built on "both-and".

- You may make negative assumptions because of the history of your relationship with the other person. It's as if the other person can't ever tell you anything new because you have already written the script. You then treat your own views and assumptions as immutable facts rather than the personal frame of existence that they are.

In any kind of confrontation or negotiation, see the other party as if for the first time. Use your eyes, ears and feelings afresh to capture what is happening in the present. Stay in the now, and gently deter your thoughts from drifting to past injuries or future negative imaginings.

To help you handle the situation well, replace unhelpful assumptions with positive ones:

1. **Assume the other person has a positive intention**
   However unacceptable the behaviour, they are trying to achieve an intention that makes sense to them. For example:

- Their strong desire to get a task done might be the "good" intention that underlies overbearing and bullying behaviour.
- A "good" desire to be acknowledged by other people may result in unpleasant attention-seeking behaviour.
- A "good" desire to do things correctly may make the person picky and pedantic.
- A "good" intention to look competent may result in face-saving behaviour and deceit.

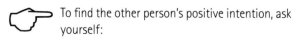

If you can intuit a person's underlying positive intention you hold the key to understanding their motivation and getting the outcome you want. Curiosity is what is needed here. Instead of criticism and condemnation, try the spirit of enquiry.

To find the other person's positive intention, ask yourself:

- What does the other person get out of this negative behaviour?
- How are they interpreting this situation?
- What matters to them in this? What does it do for them?
- Which of their values may I be trampling on in this situation?

If you can let go of your own certainties a little and move towards an attitude of curiosity you will discover positive ways to proceed.

2. Assume that you have what is needed to deal with the situation

- Remind yourself that a life without differences and disagreements doesn't exist! Ask yourself what will give you the highest chance of helping and the least chance of doing harm in this situation.
- Remind yourself that the truth is ultimately best for both parties. Continuing with important issues not faced, bad performance unmentioned, irritation not aired or lies not confronted just perpetuates a state of affairs that is negative and stuck.
- Remind yourself of your trust in yourself – that you are okay, competent, deserving and sufficient to the task. You are all of that.

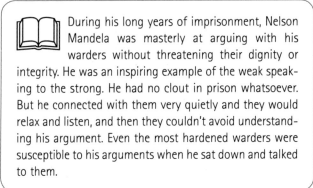

During his long years of imprisonment, Nelson Mandela was masterly at arguing with his warders without threatening their dignity or integrity. He was an inspiring example of the weak speaking to the strong. He had no clout in prison whatsoever. But he connected with them very quietly and they would relax and listen, and then they couldn't avoid understanding his argument. Even the most hardened warders were susceptible to his arguments when he sat down and talked to them.

3. Assume success

Take on the belief that there are always things to agree about; it's just a matter of extending those areas of agreement. When you assume positive intention on the part of the other party, you can find out what matters to them. For example, if you ask one faction in a violent conflict, "What do you want?" the exchange might go like this:

What do you want?
More arms and military equipment.
What is your positive intention in acquiring more arms?
To protect the population.
And what is your positive intention in protecting the population?
Everyone's safety.

Eventually you reach a statement with which you both agree and that becomes your starting place for negotiation.

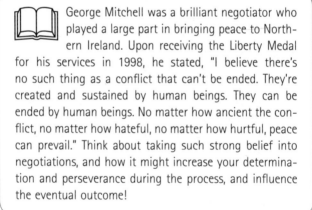

George Mitchell was a brilliant negotiator who played a large part in bringing peace to Northern Ireland. Upon receiving the Liberty Medal for his services in 1998, he stated, "I believe there's no such thing as a conflict that can't be ended. They're created and sustained by human beings. They can be ended by human beings. No matter how ancient the conflict, no matter how hateful, no matter how hurtful, peace can prevail." Think about taking such strong belief into negotiations, and how it might increase your determination and perseverance during the process, and influence the eventual outcome!

14.3 Taking the initiative

So, having taken into consideration *how* to approach conflict issues, what do you actually say when you want to confront someone personally? You'll find it helpful to include each of the following elements:

- Identify the specific issue without any interpretation or evaluation of motives. Use personal language for your own part in it: "I saw", "I heard", "X told me" etc.
- Voice your own perceptions of the behaviour, making it clear that they are your own personal interpretation/meaning: "It seems to me", "It appears to me", "It felt to me that".
- Invite the other person to tell their side of the story, listening carefully with respect and inviting them to join you in finding the truth. "What happened from your point of view?"
- Whatever the response, stay firm and positive in your intention to move towards a resolution of the situation.
- Explain what you'd like to happen as a result of your conversation. Don't assume that you can change the other person's mind, but your mutual understanding of the different points of view will help you reach a result that satisfies both of you.
- Check finally that you are both in agreement about the way forward.

Here's an example, pared down to its basics:

- "When you suggested to the board that I wasn't interested in leading the project, my perception was that you were deliberately trying to humiliate me."
- "How do you see what happened?" (Listen and respond.)
- "You've explained that you didn't mean to give that impression. So I'd like to ask you to put the account straight at the next meeting, and explain that the suggestion I wasn't interested didn't come from me."

Then you seek agreement and move into your concluding remarks.

 The power of confrontation lies in its simplicity, and in *how* you connect with the person as you say what needs to be said.

Stay flexible and quick on your feet – you can't just stick rigidly to this or any other prepared text. Really listen and respond to the other person's replies. Ask open questions. Acknowledge what you can – for example, the other person's right to perceive things as they see them, their right to their feelings and their personal set of values. And also acknowledge to yourself that you can't know exactly what the other person is thinking or feeling or why they think and feel as they do.

Once you feel confident to address issues as they arise, you will probably discover just how many opportunities you've missed in the past through not wanting to confront people. All the breaches of trust, withheld information, incompetence, missed promises, deceits, sub-standard performance, rudeness . . . When you feel confident to deal with issues while they're still small, you're much more in control of your life.

Part 4

Creative Conversations

15

CHANGING THE WORLD ONE CONVERSATION AT A TIME

> *"Remember that what gets talked about and how it gets talked about determines what will happen. Or won't happen. And that we succeed or fail, gradually then suddenly, one conversation at a time."*
> – Susan Scott

What we talk about and how we talk about it matters. Honest, energized conversations are the way to change the world. That's how it has always happened.

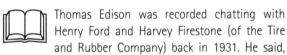 Thomas Edison was recorded chatting with Henry Ford and Harvey Firestone (of the Tire and Rubber Company) back in 1931. He said, "We should be using Nature's inexhaustible sources of energy – sun, wind and tide . . . I'd put my money on the sun and solar energy. What a source of power! I hope we don't have to wait until oil and coal run out before we tackle that." This is how ideas build momentum – a conversation here, a conversation there – especially when the speakers have influence.

15.1 Scientific advances

Whenever talented people are thrown together, ideas are born and grow. Almost 500 years ago, informal conversations sprang up in London in new coffee houses where men met to discuss the future of society and politics. Their influence became so powerful that they were shut down for a while in the eighteenth century when the government of the day felt threatened. Conversation has always been the crucible for new thinking, and many new ideas emerged from coffee house discussions, including the founding of the Royal Society, a great supporter of innovation. At Royal Society gatherings, a fascinating cross-section of famous thinkers, including Benjamin Franklin, Isaac Newton and Karl Marx, discussed ideas of the day.

Some of the most important recent discoveries in science have come about through conversations between different disciplines, both in funded ventures and outside formal channels. The discovery of DNA resulted from conversations between Crick, a biophysicist, and Watson, a biologist. MRI scanning became possible through the coming together of an American chemist, Paul Lauterbur and an English physicist, Peter Mansfield. The whole area of cognitive science – combining psychology, linguistics, computer science, philosophy and neurobiology, with the help of medical PET scans and CAT scans – is a huge conversation between scientists from different fields. Interdisciplinary research is now given prominence in many universities.

You might say that Silicon Valley owes its entire existence to a private conversation between eight frustrated, energetic and creative young men in 1957. They were all working at the time for the Nobel Prize winning, but impossible, boss, William Shockley, and all were demotivated. One evening, downhearted, the "traitorous eight" met at the house of one of them to talk about what to do next. Without any very clear idea, they made the decision to find some way to work together as a group. Later, they met up with advisors who told them about a novel idea called venture capital, which eventually gave them the backing to start their own company. If you trace back, that first conversation of the eight brilliant but disgruntled employees eventually left a legacy of several hundred companies in Silicon Valley and a trail of world-changing inventions including laptops, ATMs and iPhones.

Conversation is about connection in more than one sense. When two or more people connect in conversation, they often make intuitive creative connections that spark new ideas.

Dr Rafat Ansari, a scientist doing research for NASA, was talking to his father who suffered from cataracts when he suddenly made an important connection. He was working at that time with fluid physics experiments conducted by astronauts in space, which included work with small particles suspended in liquids. In a flash of insight, he suddenly realized that his father's eye disease was also about small particles suspended in liquids, and wondered if an instrument being developed as part of the NASA experiment might be able to detect cataracts, possibly earlier than ever before. He followed up his hunch, and the instrument is now used to assess the effectiveness of new therapies for early stages of cataract development, and has been adapted to identify other eye diseases, diabetes and possibly even Alzheimer's.

Oxford dons of very different subjects found an important link between the unlikely bedfellows of space science and archaeology through the glorious serendipity of a casual common-room conversation. As a result, multispectral imaging methods developed by NASA for seeing and understanding the Martian surface were applied to some badly charred Roman manuscripts, found buried by the Vesuvius eruption of AD 79. The space technology made the ancient material readable for the first time. Now the same process is being used to examine formerly illegible Egyptian finds, including plays of Sophocles and Euripides, poems of Pindar and Sappho, and a gospel of Thomas thought by some to be more authentic than the New Testament Gospels. Who would have thought of making *that* connection?

15.2   Political change

History shows us that political conversation has power. We read of battles and wars, treaties and taxes; but, as Hilary Mantel points out in *Wolf Hall*, change happens through conversations: "The fate of peoples is made like this, two men in small rooms. Forget the coronations, the conclaves of cardinals, the pomp and processions. This is how the world changes." An empire collapses, a war is averted; a new nation is born without bloodshed; behind many of the extraordinary changes in the world lie private conversations between people of influence or even private individuals.

In South Africa in 1989, with Nelson Mandela still in prison, F. W. de Klerk became leader of the National Party and cordially invited Mandela to tea. The two men connected: de Klerk said that his purpose in that first meeting was to get to know Mandela, and he found a man whose integrity he could trust, with an aura of calmness and authority. "I sort of liked him," he said. Change becomes possible when people connect and find they share values. That first conversation spelled the beginning of the end of apartheid. Six weeks after their meeting, de Klerk became president and unconditionally released most ANC prisoners. After further "friendly" meetings with Mandela, he released him and legalized all formerly banned political parties. The new South Africa was born.

Sometimes a conversation takes place almost by accident to change the course of history.

One May day in 1983, Canadian former cabinet minister Eugene Whelan was very late to a dinner party he had organized for Soviet Union dignitaries including Mikhail Gorbachev and Aleksandr Yakovlev, the Soviet Ambassador to Canada. It was a period in which the Cold War was at its most icy; President Reagan had just referred to the USSR as "that evil empire". Gorbachev and Yakovlev decided to take a walk while they waited for their host. "At first we kind of sniffed around each other and our conversation didn't touch on serious issues," claimed Yakovlev later. And then, gradually, in a conversation that lasted three hours, they somehow threw caution to the winds and became very frank and open with each other. They poured out all their hopes and fears, and came to agreement on a number of main points that sowed the seeds of *perestroika* and *glasnost*. Very shortly after their chat, Yakovlev was invited back home to the USSR to take charge of the Institute of World Economy and International Relations. When Gorbachev became head of the Soviet Union a couple of years later, Yakovlev became of one of his chief advisors in implementing *perestroika* and *glasnost*.

How did it happen? Certainly it needed time for them to get to know and trust each other. Certainly, the situation was so bad that eventually they showed their true emotions and spoke from the heart. Maybe both realized that through serendipity they had been thrown a now-or-never opportunity.

15.3 Voice of the people

"Never doubt that a small group of thoughtful committed citizens can change the world; indeed, it is the only thing that ever has."
– Margaret Mead

When nations allow democratic conversations, change is inevitable. No wonder free conversation is the first thing to go in a dictatorship. Maybe it is impossible to silence talk completely. Cicero claimed that conversation, being so transient, was impossible to censor and the essence of free speech.

The American Revolution was simmering away in sewing-circle chat across America well before the War of Independence. The principles of the constitution were created first in committees of correspondence that grew up organically across the continent. In France, revolutionary fervour in Paris grew from conversations outside in the cafés and inside in the salons well before it exploded into popular revolt. Listen to the conversations of today and you can predict tomorrow.

In our own day, conversation has gone global. For the first time in history we can create conversations about issues at the heart of our human existence and they spread at high speed around the planet. While politicians in their parliaments are often still posturing and sticking to party lines or vote-winning arguments, passionate people across the globe are creating important conversations using new technologies. They are listening to each other, touching and influencing each other, and joining forces to create a better world.

Every great environmental campaign or social change starts with a conversation between a very few people. The conversation opens anywhere – in people's homes, in offices, cafés and pubs, or in virtual space. As a result of the conversation, people come together with passion and more people join in to create change.

Such conversations are possible when they adopt the best aspects of face-to-face conversations – becoming curious about each other, listening actively, speaking with courtesy, allowing vulnerability, seeking to connect and understand. If we wish to avoid the violence and massive inequality of our century, it's of the utmost importance to keep the conversation going – to overcome our fears and keep the channel open between us; to be willing always to engage in dialogue.

Online discussions are gaining momentum due to social media. One powerful example is the Alliance to End Slavery and Trafficking, which has brought together 12 different human rights organizations in the USA, who are able to work collaboratively partly as the result of social media. Another is Avaaz, a global web movement with more that 28 million members, bringing the voice of ordinary people to political decision-making everywhere. TED Conversations, linked to the highly successfully TED Talks, provide a social media platform for online conversations with a time limit to keep them focused and meaningful. Currently they have more than 15 million monthly users.

The world has always changed through conversations between people who care and think something matters enough to take steps together to change the status quo. This applies to climate change and world peace and it applies equally to family harmony and children's happiness. When you get to know someone personally, through conversation, you are forced to recognize your common humanity. It's the opposite of drones, a deadly technology that obscures humanity.

Conversation is all about connection, and we connect most easily when we speak at the level of heart and soul. At the level of places, possessions and activities we live in vastly different conditions and do many different things, but we're all human; all experience human feelings and share human values. Bridges can be built through common aspirations.

Through connection with each other, we make creative connections and spot opportunities and explore possibilities. "Only connect," said Margaret in E. M. Forster's *Howard's Way*, referring not only to building loving relations, but also to joining up the dots, using both "prose and passion" in our relations with each other.

15.4 One personal conversation at a time

"The core act of leadership must be the act of making conversations real."
– David Whyte

In the final analysis, it doesn't really matter whether it's a conversation with a son, mother, friend, with a dying person or for a cause large or small – it's the *nature* of a conversation that counts. In the end, there *are* no small conversations – everyone has the potential to increase understanding and connection. Everything becomes possible when I see your humanity and you see mine and we appreciate that we are the same. Every conversation of ruler and ruled, boss and employee, partner and partner, mother and child, teacher and student, stranger and stranger – every single conversation has huge potential.

Potential needs time. When we meet someone, most of us have a strong instinct to say something or do something, and we rush outward to meet the other person in words, or rush inward to wonder what to say. But conversation is more about being than doing. If we allow space – to breathe, to look, to feel, to think and to be – the connection and conversation come to us in the silence without any conscious effort on our part. Knowing that, we can choose to open our eyes and see. It's fascinating how, as our conversation changes, so the people around us change, and then the possibilities change. We become attractors for a different kind of person and a different level of dialogue.

And the world changes – one conversation at a time.

ABOUT THE AUTHOR

Judy Apps is an international communication specialist, coach, author and inspirational speaker. A Professional Certified Coach of the International Coaching Federation and a fully qualified member of the NLP University Global Trainers' and Consultants' Network, she coaches people from every walk of life in communication, confidence and voice. In her popular "Voice of Influence" open programmes her intuitive way of connecting with people's inner potential has enabled hundreds of people to achieve great leaps in their communication and personal confidence.

Judy is author of *Voice of Influence*, a fascinating mind–body approach to finding your powerful authentic voice; *Butterflies and Sweaty Palms*, offering highly effective strategies for all who are daunted by public speaking; and *Voice and Speaking Skills For Dummies*, a comprehensive guide in this practical series. In *The Art of Conversation*, she touches the very heart of what it means to communicate. Change your conversation and you transform your life.

IMAGE CREDITS

INDEX

abstract terms   35
accents   157
Action Talk   124–7, 140, 150, 152
Alas Smith and Jones   27–8
Alliance to End Slavery and
      Trafficking   222
American Revolution   221
Amos, Tori   13
anecdotes   75–7
      see also stories
Angelou, Maya   133
anger   202
Ansari, Rafat   217
anxiety   49–50, 53, 176
argumentativeness   138
articulation   158
artificial intelligence   13–14
assumptions   64, 86, 204–8
attitude   101, 102
      see also state of mind
Austen, Jane   130
authenticity   113, 142, 168
Avaaz   222
awareness   59, 78

banter   104, 131–2
being present in the moment   48,
      59–61

being seen   142
Berlin, Isaiah   15
Berne, Eric   194
body language   13, 155–6, 163–5
      changing talk-types   153
      connection   37–8, 41
      disagreement   198, 199, 200, 201
      emotions   166, 168
      feedback   181
      listening   90, 91–2
      status games   189, 190
breathing   52–3, 169, 173–4, 176,
      203
      changes with mood   163
      listening   97, 165
      noticing other people's   38, 41
      using your voice   158, 160
Brown, Brene   41
Brown, T. Graham   163
Bunker, Archie   21
Burnett, Mark   4
"buzz"   135

calmness   51, 167, 176
capabilities, asking about   129–30
change   113, 215, 219–20, 221–2,
      224
changing the subject   74

children 3, 62, 85, 114–15
Churchill, Winston 16, 35, 79
Cicero 17, 147, 221
clues, conversational 77–8
coaching 4, 79, 112
Cohen, Andy 77
Coleridge, Samuel 15
comments, making 66–7, 68–9,
    179–80
common ground 32–4
common language 35–6
common purpose 103
competitiveness 76, 125, 188
confidence 142
confident ignorance 175
conflict 198, 208
confrontation 201–11
    see also disagreement
connection 18–19, 21–2, 47–8,
    222–3, 224
    breaking 45–6, 48
    common ground 32–4
    common language 35–6
    curiosity 63
    deep listening 97
    despite disagreement 198–9
    emotional truth 141
    energetic 41–2
    flexibility 43–5
    influence grown through 115
    knowing your intention 103
    leading through 107–9
    non-verbal 37–40, 41
    "radiators" 31
    rapport 162
    silence 61
    Soul Talk 147, 148, 149
    trust 64
content of conversations 18, 19
controversial subjects 73

conversational clues 77–8
conversational "drains" 23–31, 47
conversationalists 15
Crick, Francis 123, 216
criticism 88
cultural differences 198
curiosity 42, 62–3, 78, 93, 206,
    222

Dahl, Roald 204–5
dance, conversation as a 12–13, 15,
    16, 21
daydreaming 84
De Klerk, F.W. 219
De Los Santos, Marisa 11
De Quincey, Thomas 15
De Staël, Mme 12
debate 130, 131
deep listening 96–7
dialogue 4, 12, 197, 222, 224
Diogenes 79
disagreement 197–200, 201
    see also confrontation
disconnecting 45–6
Disraeli, Benjamin 157
diversion 89
DNA 4, 123, 216
Dowling, Tim 167
"drains" 23–31, 47
drifting off 84
Dyke, Greg 184

Echo-bores 27–8
Edison, Thomas 215
education 3
Ego-bores 28–9
Einstein, Albert 148, 149
Eliot, George 28
Eliot, T.S. 50, 141
embarrassment 11, 107, 141, 163

emotional support   137
emotional truth   141
emotions/feelings   13, 34, 58, 153, 168
  confrontation   202–3, 210
  expressing yourself   166–7
  Heart Talk   133–41
  language use   36
  listening   90, 96
  tone of voice   161
empathy   39, 92, 111, 131–2, 136
employees, chatting to   184–5, 186
ending a conversation   46–7
energy   23, 41–2, 107, 166, 199, 200
enjoyment   2, 56–7, 103, 105, 135–6
Enthuso-bores   23–6
entrainment   42
equality   12, 87, 174
exchange of ideas   130
external focus   59–61
eyes/eye contact   90, 145, 163, 165, 189

facial expressions   163, 164
facts   122, 123
faking it   175
families   88, 117–18, 144–5
fear   49, 50, 52, 60, 139, 169, 202
feedback   181
feelings/emotions   13, 34, 58, 153, 168
  confrontation   202–3, 210
  expressing yourself   166–7
  Heart Talk   133–41
  language use   36
  listening   90, 96
  tone of voice   161
fillers, useless   160

filtering the communication   86, 87
flexibility   43–5, 162, 178, 210
flow
  being in   97
  going with the   43–5
  speaking with   158–9
focusing on the positive   110–12
focusing outside yourself   59–61
Forster, E.M.   223
French Revolution   221
friends   18–19, 105, 117–18, 122–3, 135
Fry, Stephen   16
fun   2, 122

games   47, 88–9, 187–95
Gandhi, Mahatma   50
generative conversations   148–9
gestures   37, 90, 145, 163, 164
Getz, Stan   13
Gibran, Kahlil   201
global conversations   221
Gorbachev, Mikhail   22, 220
gossip   29, 31, 34
Grahame, Kenneth   124
group conversations   126

habitual thoughts   144–5
Hafiz   95
Hale, Shannon   49
Hazlitt, William   79
Head Talk   128–32, 140, 150, 152
Heart Talk   133–41, 150–1, 152
Hessler, Peter   147
humour   73, 122, 126
  see also wit

ideas, exchanging   130
"if", using the word   111–12

influence   3, 101–15
  emotions   166–7
  knowing your intention   103–6
  leading through connection
    107–9
  positive sensor   110–12
  stories   113–15
  two-way   149
information, finding out   103, 121,
  126–7
initiative, taking the   209–11
intellectual stimulation   105, 130
intention   42, 101–2, 103–6, 108,
  113
  magnet metaphor   112
  positive assumptions   205–6
  Soul Talk   146, 148
interest   24, 27, 109, 179–80
  expressing   160–2
  Heart Talk   136
  listening   86
  shared   32–3, 122–3
  stories   75
internal voice   59
interruptions   17, 45, 83, 89
intimate conversation   137–40, 146,
  147–8
introducing yourself   69–70
Izzard, Eddie   13

Johnstone, Keith   187, 189
Jones, Griff Rhys   27–8
judgement   87–8, 89
Jung, Carl   149, 166

Kabir   155
keeping a conversation going
  71–4
King, Martin Luther   35

language
  awareness of your own   139
  common   35–6
  emotional support   137
  negative   110–11
  personal   209
Lauterbur, Paul   216
leadership   162, 224
Leonard, Thomas   101
Linklater, Kirsten   142
listening   5, 12, 13, 16, 41, 79–97
  Action Talk   125
  being present in the moment
    60
  body language   37, 165
  confrontation   209, 210
  daydreaming instead of   84
  deep listening   96–7
  feedback   181
  filtering the communication   86
  freeing yourself to listen   93–5
  judgement   87–8
  non-listening   85–6
  pretending to listen   85
  reassuring or diverting   89
  rehearsing instead of   82–3
  showing that you're listening
    91–2
  skills   81
  to sounds   167
loyalty   184, 185

Mandela, Nelson   50, 207, 219
manipulation   108, 191–2
Mann, Thomas   7
Mansfield, Peter   216
Mantel, Hilary   219
McCafferty, Megan   25
Mead, Margaret   221

meaning   90, 133, 146, 148, 155–6, 162, 164
meetings   45
memories   56–8, 114
metaphors   115, 143–4
mind games   88–9
  see also games
mirroring   21, 37, 38, 199
Mitchell, George   208
Moaning Mickeys and Minnies 29–31
monosyllables   67, 71–2
Monroe, Marilyn   50
Montaigne, Michel de   197
mood   42, 51, 163, 167
movement   37, 53–5, 90, 145, 163, 164–5
MRI scanning   216
muscle memory   58
musicians   13

naming the game   195
negative assumptions   205
negative attitudes   23, 29–31
negative language   110–11
nervousness   27, 50, 59, 176
Nesbitt, Kenn   120
networking   3, 27, 119
nods and grunts   92, 181
non-listening   85–6
non-verbal communication   37–40, 41, 82, 90, 91–2, 181
  see also body language

objects of attention   33–4
old games   193–4
online discussions   222
open questions   73–4, 210
openness   105, 153, 185

opinions   13, 128, 129, 130–1, 139
Osho   168

Pacino, Al   198
pauses   160
  see also silence
personal information, revealing   78, 131
persuasion   3, 131
  see also influence
Picoult, Jodi   85
pitch, varying your   158
Plato   130
politeness   26
politics   4, 219–20
positive assumptions   64, 205–6
positive sensor   110–12
positive state of mind   56–8, 104, 173–4
Postman, Neil   125
posture   38, 90, 91, 163
power plays   188, 189
pretending to listen   85
problematic conversations   172–81
prompting   180
purpose, common   103

QI   16
Queen of Gossip   29
questions
  Action Talk   124, 126, 151
  answering unasked questions 47
  confrontation   210
  flexibility   178
  gaining trust   115
  Head Talk   128–30, 152
  Heart Talk   133–4, 136, 138, 140, 151, 152

keeping a conversation going 71–4
listening 92
moving the conversation forward 174
positive 110–12
prompting 180
Robo-chores 26
rules of the game 177
Soul Talk 143, 148
speaking with flow 158–9
starting a conversation 67–8, 69
Thing Talk 120, 121–2
"Yes but" game 193–4

"radiators" 23, 31, 101
rapport 18, 162
reassurance 89
rehearsing 82–3
relationships 2, 183–4, 186, 200
relaxation 51, 52–3, 54, 93, 158, 160
respect 13, 42
risk taking 140–1
Robo-chores 26–7
role playing 183–6
Roosevelt, Eleanor 128
Royal Society 216
rules of the game 177
Rumi 147, 162

salespeople 191–2
Salwei, Patricia 146–7
scientific discoveries 3–4, 123, 216–18
Scott, Susan 215
self-consciousness 49–50, 52, 59, 169
self-disclosure 78, 131
self-presentation 168

senses 57, 59, 60
Shakespeare, William 132
Shaw, George Bernard 12
shyness 50, 70, 139
silence 61, 115, 146, 147, 179, 224
Silicon Valley 216–17
skin colour 38, 90, 145, 163
small talk 69, 126–7
Smith, Mel 27–8
social media 222
Socrates 3
soft focus 96
Soul Talk 142–9, 151, 152
South Africa 219
speed of talking 40, 46, 47, 157, 158, 160, 176
spiritual questions 148
Starbird, Michael 44
starting a conversation 65–70
    asking a question 67–8, 69
    introducing yourself 69–70
    making a comment 66–7, 68–9
state of mind 49–64, 115
    curiosity 62–3
    dealing with silence 61
    focusing outside yourself 59–61
    influencing others 107
    listening 93, 94
    managing your 51–5
    positive 56–8, 104, 173–4
    skin colour changes 163
    trust 64
status games 187–90
stopping talking 176
    see also ending a conversation
stories 75–7, 113–15, 124–5
strangers, talking with 65, 69, 147
subjects
    building trust 115
    changing the subject 74

common ground   32–3
controversial   73
Head Talk   128–9
people's preferences   33–4
Thing Talk   120–3
subtlety   13, 115
synchronicity   42

TED Conversations   222
Temple, William   3
tension   49, 52, 54, 59, 90, 93, 107, 176
Thatcher, Margaret   22
Thing Talk   120–3, 126, 150, 152
thoughts   13, 56–8, 128, 129, 159, 168
tone of voice   39–40, 90, 161–2
changing talk-types   152–3
disagreement   198, 199, 200, 201
dull   84
emotions   166, 168
ending a conversation   46, 47
Heart Talk   140
influence   115
meaning expressed through   155
noticing other people's   13, 41, 145
trust   64
building   78, 115, 185
controversial subjects   73
curiosity   63
gaining   142
good connection   21
Heart Talk   134
values about   104, 105
truth, emotional   141
Turing test   13–14
types of conversation   117–53
Action Talk   124–7, 140, 150, 152
Head Talk   128–32, 140, 150, 152

Heart Talk   133–41, 150–1, 152
progressing through   150–3
Soul Talk   142–9, 151, 152
Thing Talk   120–3, 126, 150, 152

unconscious mind   149
useless fillers   160

values   86, 104–6, 134, 135, 210
voice, expressing yourself with your   157–62
voice tone   39–40, 90, 161–2
changing talk-types   152–3
disagreement   198, 199, 200, 201
dull   84
emotions   166, 168
ending a conversation   46, 47
Heart Talk   140
influence   115
meaning expressed through   155
noticing other people's   13, 41, 145
vulnerability, accepting your   60–1, 139, 169, 222

Watson, James   123, 216
Whyte, David   200, 224
Wilde, Oscar   172
win-win outcomes   204
Winfrey, Oprah   23, 101
wit   15, 16, 131–2
see also humour
Wodehouse, P.G.   65
Woolf, Virginia   15–16
workplaces   3, 117–18, 130, 183–6

Yakovlev, Aleksandr   220
"Yes but" game   193–4